JOHN DIXON
LLINGTON HO

MINERS ASSOCIATION
RYHOPE LODGE

The Coalminers of Durham

Norman Emery

with a foreword by
David Guy
President of the
Durham Mineworkers' Association

ALAN SUTTON PUBLISHING LIMITED

COUNTY DURHAM BOOKS

First published in the United Kingdom in 1992
Alan Sutton Publishing Ltd
Phoenix Mill • Far Thrupp • Stroud • Gloucestershire

First published in the United States of America in 1992
Alan Sutton Publishing Inc • Wolfeboro Falls • NH 03896–0848

Paperback edition, with corrections, first published 1994
in association with County Durham Books,
publishing imprint of Durham County Council

British Library Cataloguing in Publication Data applied for

Emery, Norman
Durham Miners
I. Title
942.86
ISBN 0–7509–0030–X

Library of Congress Cataloging in Publication Data applied for

Typeset in 11/13 Times.
Typesetting and origination by
Alan Sutton Publishing Limited.
Printed in Great Britain by
WBC Limited, Bridgend.

Contents

Foreword

This book describes the development of the mining industry in County Durham and how the communities coped and struggled to improve their social and economic well-being. The many mining tragedies endured are graphically portrayed, giving an insight into the horror and sadness of the plight of the victims and their families. The bravery and comradeship displayed on these occasions by colleagues and rescuers reflect the character of those associated with the industry. The major roles played by the Durham Miners' Association, the Mining Federation of Great Britain and the National Union of Mineworkers are featured and the book demonstrates the loyalty of miners to their union and the degrees of hardship and suffering which they have endured, struggling for decent wages and conditions of employment and the principle of the right to work.

In 1884, during the eviction of miners from their homes in Silksworth, Lord Londonderry said: 'I want to teach a lesson to the deluded and obstinate victims of designing men and crafty Attorneys and to defeat the insane Union!' On 10 March 1985, after the year-long epic strike, Ian MacGregor, chairman of the then National Coal Board, said: 'People are now discovering the price of insubordination and insurrection and, boy, are we going to make it stick!' With denationalization approaching, the courage, determination and unity shown by miners in the past and depicted by Norman Emery in his book will need to be as strong as ever.

The Coalminers of Durham will, I hope, serve as an inspiration to the miners of today and those of tomorrow. With three hundred years of coal reserves under our feet in Britain, there is surely more to come!

Dave Guy

President of the Durham Mineworkers' Association

Acknowledgements

While working on this book, I have been given access to photographs, documents and books by a number of libraries and individuals, to whom I owe a debt of thanks. The following have kindly given permission for the publication of copyright material or items from special collections: Durham County Record Office; Durham County Library; Durham County Council Museum Education Service; Durham University Archives and Special Collections; South Tyneside Metropolitan Borough Council; Newcastle upon Tyne City Libraries and Arts; Easington District Council; Ryhope Community Association; the National Union of Mineworkers (Durham Area); Fillinghams; Houghall Agricultural College; the Newcastle Chronicle and Journal Ltd; and the *Sunderland Echo*.

A number of individuals have also generously given permission for me to reproduce their photographs: Mr Ray Kitching; Messrs P. and L. Hughes; Mrs Judy Plummer; Mr J. Thompson; Mr Alan Crooks; Mr Roger Norris; Mr W. Longstaffe; Mr W. Moyes; Miss J. Wade; Mr H. Wharton; Mr H. Henderson; Mr Cowburn and Mrs Lenderyou.

I am especially grateful to Mrs Mary Galloway for permission to reproduce the poems 'To Londonderry' and 'A Cross in Coal' by her late brother, Mr John Doyle. They are part of a collection of writings by a skilled poet who worked at the coalface at Horden.

Throughout my research I received invaluable help and advice from many people, and I would like to thank: the staff of Durham City Reference Library, particularly Anita, Julie and Jean; the County Archivist, Ms Jennifer Gill; Mr Jack Hedley; the staff of Beamish Museum, particularly Rosemary Allen; the National Union of Mineworkers (Durham Area); the staff of British Coal; Mr Stewart Tizard and Mr W. Garthwaite, manager and safety engineer at Dawdon Colliery; Mr K. Nightingale (manager), Mr Anthony Cain (surface superintendent), and Mr Joe Woods (surface foreman) of Murton Colliery; Mr Bill Dowding; Mr Don Wilcock; Mr Michael Wheeler; the Community Associations of Trimdon Grange, Deaf Hill and Wingate; Mr Gordon Penman of the Durham Aged Mineworkers Homes Association; Mr Roger Norris; Revd Kevin Dunn of Holy Trinity, South Hetton; Mr George Stewart; Mr Clarke; Mr A.G. Hughes, editor of the *Sunderland Echo*; Mr D. Abbott; Ms Pat Francis, librarian to the Labour Party and Mrs Barbara Heathcote.

I would also like to thank Mr Trevor Woods for his skilful copying of original photographs.

Most importantly I would like to thank my parents for their help, advice and encouragement throughout the research and writing of this book.

Introduction

In Durham coal was king. It fuelled the Industrial Revolution and played a major role in Britain's export trade. The 'black diamonds' were won by the hard labour of thousands of men and boys working in dimly lit stalls and roadways deep below the ground. It was a heavy, physical, task, in dusty, often wet, places, where there was the constant threat of roof collapse or explosion. In the period between 1869 and 1953 there were 52 explosions in the county, with the loss of 850 lives. To take one year, 1960, 185 men were injured and 30 were killed, principally through being buried by falls of ground, or by accidents during the haulage process. In every village, too, there were the men whose lungs were filled with dust, continually gasping for air.

The miner lived in a house supplied by the colliery owner, in a village where the pithead was the dominant feature. In every village there were the familiar features of mining life – the miners walking home from work, their faces blackened with coal dust, the sound of the pit hooter, the sight of the pulley-wheels turning, the 'crakeman' reporting the times of a union meeting, or the 'caller' tapping on the window to wake the miner for his shift.

In the nineteenth century the population of the villages tended to be youthful, reflecting high fertility and mortality. The miner was also highly mobile; but stable, close-knit communities developed in the terraced rows by the pit. There was a communal spirit, where people helped each other out, particularly through the dark days of strikes, short working, or 'starvation wages'. The system of work also developed close ties, particularly with the marrowing system, where a hewer worked the stall one shift, and his 'marra' followed him in the next, and they shared the wage. It was this same spirit of comradeship and loyalty which saw many a miner fighting in his county regiment, the Durham Light Infantry, on the fields of Flanders or the deserts of North Africa.

The brotherhood of the miner was also expressed in the union, with every pit having a union lodge. The Gala was the highlight of the miner's year, when the lodges of the union converged on Durham City, and took it over for the day. The lodge banner would be rolled up and carried with its poles to the village station (in the days when colliery villages had stations) and placed in the guard's van of the train, and most of the villagers, men, women and children, would travel into Durham. The city station is on a ridge, and once the train had pulled in, the banner would be brought out and set up on its poles as the crowd disgorged from the carriages brfore proceeding down into North Road, the main thoroughfare, into the heart of the city. Most lodges came with a band, and they would march down North Road, over Framwellgate Bridge, under the shadow of Durham Castle, and up the narrow Silver Street to the Market Place, where Gaetomo Monti's statue of Londonderry, the colliery owner, dominates the open space. Banner after banner passed him by on its way to Elvet, bands playing, and the footpaths lined with crowds of people, so many that police on horseback have to keep the route clear. On the balcony of the County Hotel leading figures of the Labour Party and trade union movement would wave to the marchers. Some years the crowds were silenced as a banner was carried forward, draped in black crape, recalling death in the pit. Onward the banners and crowds marched, to the Racecourse, in a seemingly endless procession, the banners displaying symbols of trade union loyalty, with their messages of 'Unity is Strength' and the frequently repeated depiction of the fable of the sticks, unbreakable in a bundle, but easily broken individually. Each lodge then took its banner and erected it against the enclosure fence. When all the lodges were present, the field was bordered with painted, fluttering, silk. On the Racecourse stands were erected, where the guest speakers addressed the throng. But apart from the speeches, there were the tea tents, the travelling shows, boating on the river, and the pubs, which did a roaring trade. In the afternoon the miners' service was a major attraction. The great Norman cathedral was always packed.

The Gala has, in many ways, been an indicator of the condition of coalmining in the county. As the years have gone by, and pits have closed, so the number of banners has declined. Today the Gala is only a shadow of its former self. The late nineteenth century was the heyday of the mining industry in Durham and generally throughout the British coalfields, but over the last hundred or so years the Durham coalfield has gone from being one of the leading coal-exporting and coke-manufacturing areas in Britain to an area considered peripheral to Yorkshire with its new pit at Selby, and the rich seams of the Vale of Belvoir in Leicestershire.

Since the 1960s the traditional way of life of the pit village, the methods of work, and the terminology of pitwork and coke manufacture has largely gone, and is now often only a memory. This book, in words and pictures, attempts to record that world.

CHAPTER 1

The Durham Coalfield and the Miner

Winning the Coal

When one thinks of County Durham the things which immediately spring to mind are Durham Cathedral and coalmines. Before the middle of this century pit head winding gear was a common sight in the villages of Durham, for the county was literally 'founded on coal'.

Five hundred million years ago, when Britain was largely covered by sea, volcanic activity during the Ordovician period raised up new land, particularly in the area that is now Scotland. As a result marine conditions receded southwards across England. During this gradual retreat the environment changed, with sediment deposition from the north entering a delta covering a massive area, including Durham. In this Carboniferous landscape coal forests developed, surviving until the arid conditions of the Permian period, about 280 million years ago.[1]

Within County Durham the coalfield spreads eastward from the mountain limestones of the Pennines. This demarcation is irregular, but the line runs roughly from Shotley Bridge, past Tow Law, to the area around Eggleston, in Teesdale. The eastern half of the coalfield, towards the coast, is concealed by an extensive deposition of Permian magnesian limestone. These underlying coal seams have been found to extend under the North Sea.

The Westphalian stratified seams may be divided into two main phased groups – the lower and middle coal measures. Although there is some confusion in the terminology from one mining area to another, the lower deposits comprise the Marshall Green, Victoria, Brockwell, Three-Quarter, Busty, Tilly and Harvey. The middle coal measures are made up of the Hutton, Brass Thill, Low Main, Maudlin, Yard, Main and Five-Quarter. The carbon content of these bituminous coals is particularly high, ranging from 89 to 90 per cent in the west, declining to around 86 per cent on the coast near Seaham.

The first clearly documented evidence of the mining of coal in County Durham is in the Boldon Book of 1183. This register of the Bishop of Durham's personal lands and the dues payable by his tenants records that an unnamed collier at Escomb, near Bishop Auckland, was to find coal for a smith at Coundon to make ploughs, while a smith, listed under Wearmouth and Tunstall, found his own coal supply for the forge.[2] Small mines were worked during the medieval period, particularly from the fourteenth century, with pits around the Tyne and in the valley of the River Wear.[3] The workings were probably in the form of bell pits. Two indentures, of the late fourteenth and early fifteenth century, between the Prior of Durham and John Fossour and Richard Couhird, refer to the practices and agreements of coalmining at this time. In the first indenture, the two men agreed to win coal from their pit at Broom and deliver it to the cathedral in Durham and the community at Bearpark.[4] The prior agreed not to work any of his own coal reserves during this period, on condition that the Broom workings did not damage his own pit. If the two men failed to maintain the agreed supply, and the prior was forced to buy from elsewhere, they would recompense him. The measure of coal at this time was based on the 'chaldron', which contained six 'quarters'. In the later indenture, Fossour was again allowed to work the pit at Broom, but he and the prior agreed to work their pits simultaneously, the size of the workforce being decided on by the two sides, with the combined produce sold and the income divided equally between them.[5] The agreement also required Fossour to supply free seven score chaldrons of coal. While the fourteenth-century production of coal was fairly limited in quantity, some was exported down the coast to London, and across the North Sea to the Netherlands.[6] It was not, however, until the sixteenth century that output was increased significantly in order to supply, by sea, the expanding London domestic coal market. Mining concentrated particularly in the northern part of the county, close to the Tyne, during this period, and through the seventeenth and eighteenth centuries, with some small-scale exploration further inland. A coal exchange was established at Billingsgate in 1769, with factors operating as agents for the coal and colliery owners, and dealing with the buyers.[7] Coal cartels began to operate in the northern coalfield in the eighteenth and early nineteenth centuries, with the Grand Allies and the Limitation of the Vend, to regulate the coal trade, prices, supply and demand. The Industrial Revolution resulted in a dramatic increase in coal production in Durham, particularly because of the county's reserves of household, steam, gas and coking coals. The development of wagonways and the rail network enabled coal and coke to be transported more easily, with important outlets created on the major rivers of the Tyne, Wear and Tees.

The cathedral city of Durham, set on a peninsula, with the River Wear snaking around it, was the administrative and religious centre of the county.

Its castle and narrow streets were enclosed by a medieval wall, and while many of the old timber-framed houses survived, the eighteenth and nineteenth centuries saw the spread of brick-built houses and shops north, west and east from the original confines. It was a bustling centre of trade and manufacturing, with carpet-making, organ building, tanning, brick production, milling and mustard-grinding. In the main streets, narrow back alleys and enclosed yards were the workshops of painters, mattress-makers, milliners, clay-pipe makers, whitesmiths, game-dealers and a wide range of other trades, alongside a hundred hotels, inns and beerhouses. From the fine houses around the cathedral to the decaying tenements of Fram, there was a need for household fuel, and pits were sunk in the city suburbs and surrounding area to supply their needs, as well as for shipment further afield.

Surprisingly little is actually known of the city's pits. On the eastern side of the loop of the river, in Elvet, Backhouse, Mounsey and Company had leased a site from the Dean and Chapter for a pit, some time in the first half of the nineteenth century,[8] though by the latter half of the century it had been taken over by Thomas Crawford of Littletown, purely to supply coal to the inhabitants of the city and neighbourhood.[9] In 1860 there were 300 hands employed, but by 1894 only 36 hewers were ripping coal from the Hutton seam, and working out west from the shaft as far as the fault in the Prebends Bridge area.[10] Their activities, unfortunately, affected the foundations of the historic Church of St Oswald, built in the late twelfth century, and in 1834 extensive and, apparently, tasteless restoration work was carried out there.

Close to the meandering river, east of the city, were Houghall, Shincliffe Bank Top, Old Durham and Kepier Collieries. Houghall was sunk in 1841–2 to

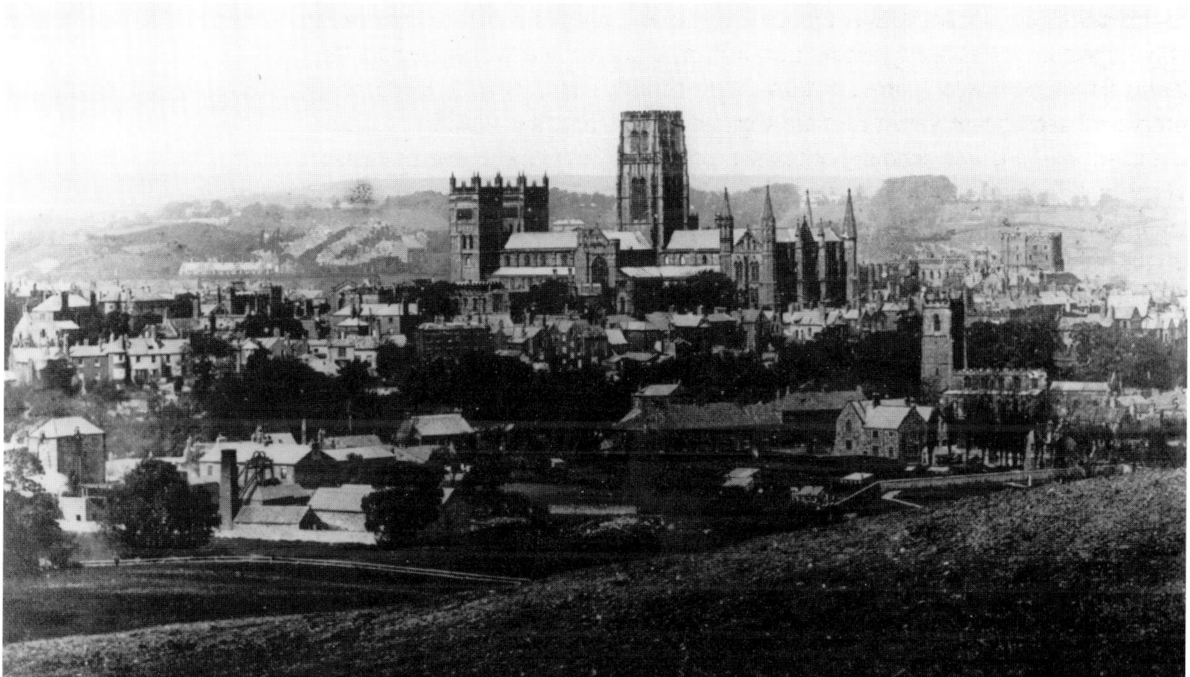

Elvet Colliery (left foreground) in the shadow of Durham Cathedral. The pit worked the Hutton seam, which was about 3 ft thick, but was abandoned in 1908.

work the Low Main and Hutton, but productivity was low, and it only survived for about forty years. Its last operator seems to have been J.H. Love and Partner.[11] Love also appears to have had links with Shincliffe, where, in fact, many of the Houghall miners lived, until houses were built at the site. By 1894 Shincliffe Pit was standing, and must have closed entirely soon afterwards.

Old Durham was worked by the Londonderry family around the 1860s, but by 1894 it had closed. In the Kepier area were the Harvey, Busty and Brockwell seams, the first two being 5 ft thick. The Kepier Grange Pit was started in 1818, though this was short-lived, and operations resumed in 1842 for several years. A new winning was started in 1873 to locate the seams on the opposite side of the river.[12] Pumps worked day and night, but at 25 fathoms the first shaft was abandoned, and when coal was found in the second shaft at 18 fathoms, it was realized that the seams in this area had thinned out due to the presence of a buried valley, and the project collapsed in 1879.

Nearby, at Crook Hall, on the west bank of the river, a pit was sunk in 1815, and, apparently, a second in 1860, which became Durham Main or Sidegate Colliery. From the 1870s to the turn of the century it was worked by J. Lishman & Company.[13] The Hutton and Low Main seams supplied coal which was sent to the city gasworks. The colliery seems to have closed in the 1920s.

To the north of the city centre were Framwellgate, Dryburn Grange, Brasside, Frankland and Grange Collieries. Framwellgate Colliery, the 'Old Pit', was started by the Northern Mining Company in 1838. Engines and 160 hp pumps were brought in, and after three years sinking through thick alluvial deposits, coal was reached. Around 140 men and boys were hired, and though they raised coal to the value of £31,000 a year, the sinking costs and profit margin led to the company's collapse later in the 1840s.[14] In 1859 it was taken over by the Marchioness of Londonderry, but worked under the name of the Framwellgate Coal Company Limited. By 1894 this company was also working Dryburn Grange Colliery. This, and the Old Pit, worked the Hutton and Busty seams, half the output going to 239 beehive ovens for conversion to coke.[15] Framwellgate was one of the longest surviving city pits, the last remnants being demolished in 1925.[16] Very little is known of Brasside and Frankland, though the Grange Colliery was cleared and became the site in 1867 of the Grange Ironworks, which, among other things, made mining equipment.[17]

East of Durham City lay the concealed coalfield. The overlying deposit of limestone had been considered an impenetrable barrier to coal exploration, but from 1820 to 1850 sinking operations were carried out at a number of sites which proved workable seams of coal.

The first site was at Hetton, where a shaft was started in 1820 by the Hetton Coal Company, and the Main coal seam was reached two years later, 660 ft below the surface. Also in the 1820s Eppleton and Elemore Collieries were sunk. These were followed, in the 1830s, by collieries at South Hetton, Haswell, Thornley, Kelloe, Wearmouth, Wingate and Murton.

The limestone and underlying quicksand, with heavy feeders of water, caused serious problems at many of these sinkings. At Haswell the initial attempt revealed the presence of 216 ft of limestone, under which lay 60 ft of quicksand.[18] After the expenditure of £60,000, the project was abandoned, and it was not until 1835 that a second attempt was successful, and the coal was taken by rail to Sunderland for shipping. The pit worked for forty-seven years before being dismantled and the plant sold off.[19] Work on Wearmouth Colliery was started in 1826, but it was not completed until 1835, when the Maudlin seam was reached at 1,596 ft.[20]

The ground for Murton Colliery was broken in 1838, and, in 1840, Edward Potter, the viewer for the South Hetton Coal Company brought in 540 hp engines to break the crust of the limestone.[21] Feeders of water began to come through the limestone, but as soon as the rock was broken through, quicksand and water burst into the shaft and rose 90 ft up it. The pumps were raising 7,000 gallons a minute to cope with the inrush, but the pumps' leather buckets wore out after about two hours, and three tanyards were kept in full employment making replacement buckets. The sand in the water also resulted in a series of breakdowns, and the company stopped operations. After seeking advice from two experts, they brought in two extra pumps and installed eighteen boilers to raise sufficient steam. Now, with a total of 1,140 hp, the pumps were able to raise 10,832 gallons a minute. Eventually the shaft was 'tubbed out', and the Hutton was reached in April 1843.

Further operations were undertaken in the concealed coalfield in the 1840s, at Castle Eden, South Wingate, Trimdon, Trimdon Grange, Seaton and Lord Londonderry's Seaham Pit.

The Vane-Tempest family had coal workings in the Rainton area, west of Durham City. Following the marriage, in 1819, of Anne Vane-Tempest, Countess of Antrim, to the third Marquis of Londonderry, a soldier and plenipotentiary to the courts of Berlin and Vienna, the exploitation of coal increased.[22] In 1828 Londonderry created Seaham Harbour to improve coal shipping, which, until then, had been by keel and collier from Fatfield.[23] While the Alexandrina, Adventure, Meadows, Nicholson and Plain Pits at Rainton formed the initial hub of the operation, Londonderry, and his agent, John Buddle, expanded the coal winning, with pits around Durham City, but more particularly with the sinking of Seaham Colliery, known locally as the 'Nicky Nack'.

During the 1844 strike, and for many years afterwards, the third marquis was attacked for evicting the miners at Seaham when they had appealed to him to mediate in the dispute, for introducing Irish strike-breakers, and for warning Seaham shopkeepers against supplying food to those he had evicted.[24] The image smeared the family name, and has persisted. It is voiced in the words of John Doyle (1900–77), a hewer at Horden:

> His Lordship reached three score and ten,
> A very fine performance when
> One thinks how many did him scorn
> And wished him dead 'ere he was born.[25]

The statue of the 3rd Marquis of Londonderry in Durham Market Place.

Despite the presence of coal beneath much of the county, few of the principal landowners actually got into the business of coalmining. Several were happy to let mining companies, created by industrialists and entrepreneurs, work the coal on lease, while receiving royalties and wayleave rights. Apart from Londonderry the only other major aristocratic landowning family which became heavily involved in winning coal was the Lambtons, whose seat was at Lambton Castle, near Chester-le-Street.

The first Earl of Durham, John George Lambton, known as 'Radical Jack', was both a colliery owner and a leading figure in British politics.[26] He was involved with the 1832 reform movement, served as ambassador to Russia, and during his time as High Commissioner of British North America he saw the union of the provinces. John George Lambton, the third earl, was a keen horseman, and steward of the Jockey Club, as well as being closely involved with the army, having held the position of lieutenant in the Coldstream Guards.[27]

The Lambtons worked the Lady Ann, the Margaret, Dorothea, 'D' Pit, Herrington, Houghton and Lumley Sixth Pit. They also had engineering works, making locomotives and stationary engines, at Philadelphia. These operations were, however, taken over by Sir James Joicey in 1896.

The rich supplies of west Durham coal and limestone also tempted a number of ironmasters to exploit local ore reserves, initially, in the 1840s, in west Durham, and from the 1850s in Cleveland. The main centres of production were at Consett, Tow Law, Witton Park, Ferryhill and later along the Tees at Middlesbrough.

Clay ironstone from the local coal measures was initially worked by the Consett Iron Company, which had been formed in 1840 with an input of £10,000 from four men, three of whom were Quakers. Two blast-furnaces were built, and additional funding permitted the erection of rolling mills. Following moves by the Redesdale Iron Company, the two firms merged under the title of the Derwent Iron Company in 1841.[28] Eleven years after the establishment of the company, the working of the local ore ceased; some was brought from the Hollins mines of the Rosedale Mining Company, but increasingly ironstone came from Upleatham. This was more economically viable, as the production of a ton of local ore cost 10s. compared with 7s. from Upleatham (including carriage).

The company had a very diverse product range, and the input of capital, from the initial pump-prime to continued investment in plant, was raised through bank credit. This credit was given by the Northumberland and Durham District Bank, and continued to be given, without, it would seem, any careful examination of trends in the iron trade, and of the company's increasingly unprofitable situation. As a result of massive debts, the bank collapsed. Various stages of negotiations led to a group of the bank creditors purchasing the works, and establishing it, in 1864, as the Consett Iron Company Limited.[29] The new company became more streamlined, shedding uneconomic plant, and increasing output by gradually demolishing the original eighteen blast-furnaces and replacing them with six new towers.

In Weardale Charles Attwood began operations in the Stanhope area in 1844, but soon afterwards moved to Tow Law, a site on the divide between the coal measures and mountain limestones, and formed the Weardale Iron Company, with finance from the London bankers, the Baring Brothers.[30] Four furnaces were built, and by 1856 180 tons of pig-iron was being

Consett Ironworks, 1925.

produced per week.[31] Works were then established at Tudhoe in 1853, and the Stanners Close Steel Company was created by Attwood at Wolsingham in 1864. Spathose ore and brown siliceous haematite came from the Stanhope–Rookhope area of Weardale,[32] though later supplies came from Cleveland and the Guisborough area.[33] The company took coal from Black Prince, West Thornley, Hedley Hill and Tudhoe Collieries. By 1861 Tow Law was producing steel ingot from Bessemer converters.[34]

Bolckow, Vaughan and Company also established an ironworks inland, at Witton Park in 1846. Ore supplies came from Weardale, particularly near Wolsingham and at the Bleaberry mines near Bishopley.[35] The seam at the latter mine was worked by longwall, until it was closed down in 1852. The company produced large quantities of rail and plate at their rolling mills, but increasingly from 1850 ore was being sent from the bord and pillar workings in the Eston Hills.

In 1859 James Morrison established the Ferryhill Ironworks, with two blast-furnaces using Rosedale ore.[36] In 1864 the company amalgamated with the owners of the ironstone deposits to form the Rosedale and Ferryhill Iron Company. The company had furnaces ranging from 55 ft to a massive 103 ft high tower with a 31 ft bosh, the largest in the county. The works were linked to Thrislington and Coxhoe Collieries, the latter having a coke-yard.

The need for increasing supplies of iron ore, following the decline of local reserves in the west of the county, and the problems of transporting the finished or semi-finished product, became increasingly difficult problems for the Durham ironmasters. The discovery of ironstone in the Guisborough area, and in the Eston and Upleatham Hills in the 1850s, accentuated, in many ways, these difficulties. There were rich deposits in the Middle Lias,[37] containing on average about 30 per cent metal, though it was also acidic, with a significant phosphorous content – Eston, Upleatham and Normanby ironstone, for instance, having 1.07 to 1.86 per cent phosphorous. Pig-iron with this level of phosphorous was unsuitable for steel-making, because it produced a brittle metal.

In 1879 a solution was developed by Gilchrist Thomas at Bolckow and Vaughans Works in Middlesbrough, where a Bessemer converter was lined with bricks of magnesian limestone and soda which had been baked at high temperature.[38] Into the vessel was poured Eston ordinary pig-iron; the blast was turned on, and a flux of lime and 'blue billy' was thrown in, after the silicon had been removed. Ten per cent of *Spiegeleisen* (manganese-rich pig-iron) was later added, and the resulting molten metal was ladled into ingot moulds. The result was a basic steel with only 0.03 per cent phosphorus. Consequently, the Cleveland area became a chief producer of steel, and output of iron ore reached a peak of 6.5 million tons by 1881. With the development of Middlesbrough as a port, Teesside became the centre of iron and steel production, with the river lined with the works of Bolckow, Vaughan and Company, Pease, Bernhard Samuelson and others.

The blast-furnaces on the less favourable inland sites, well away from the principal ore deposits and ports, declined as the ironmasters were attracted to the east coast. In 1875 Charles Attwood died, though the Weardale Iron Company continued to operate. Rising costs and declining output led to the closure of Tow Law in 1886, and though Tudhoe changed to open-hearth steel production, using Spanish ore, it too was closed down, and the operation moved to Cargo Fleet, at the mouth of the River Tees, following a takeover of the company by Sir Christopher Furness, a leading West Hartlepool industrialist and shipbuilder.[39] Only the Wolsingham plant survived *in situ*, with involvement in armament production, under the control of John Rogerson.[40]

Bolckow, Vaughan and Company also established, and took over, ironworks in Middlesbrough, particularly the Cleveland Ironworks and the Middlesbrough Ironworks. With this concentration of effort on the Tees, which gave access for shipping, the more isolated works at Witton Park was run down, and eventually dismantled around 1884.[41] Their Teesside works increasingly looked to the Iberian peninsula and Africa for fresh sources of ore.

With the disposal of the Derwent Iron Company's Upleatham ironstone reserves to J. and J.W. Pease, Consett Iron Company Limited began using Cumbrian ores, but as this source declined, new ore was brought in from the Bilbao Rubio mines in northern Spain around 1872/3, following mining agreements with the Dowlais Iron Company, Ybarra, and Krupps of Essen.[42] By this means, and by concentrating on the production of pig-iron and steel, Consett survived. It began open-hearth steel-making in 1882, and took coal from its pits at Westwood, Medomsley, Hunter, Eden, Blackhill, Delves, Langley Park and Garesfield.[43]

Linked to both the coal industry and the iron and steel trades, as principal consumers, were shipbuilding and heavy engineering, where output and labour force had increased dramatically in the latter half of the nineteenth century. The net registered tonnage of the Tyne, for instance, rose from 5,413 in 1861 to a peak before the Second World War of 214,713 tons in 1920, with fifteen shipbuilding yards producing warships and merchant steamers, and dry-dock facilities for ship repair.[44] Engineering also increased, with boiler-making and other marine machinery manufacture, for domestic needs, including products for use in the Clyde and Belfast shipyards, as well as for sale to Holland and Germany.

In 1913 Durham reached its highest rate of coal production, with an output of 41,533,000 tons, raised by 165,246 hands from 304 pits.[45] Exports of the county's prime gas and coking coals were principally to Germany, but also to Belgium, France and Italy. By the 1920s and '30s much of the coal production of the county was in the hands of huge combines.[46] These included Dorman Long, Pease and Partners, Lord Londonderry, the enterprises of James Joicey, and the Horden Collieries Ltd.

Dorman Long and Company Limited was formed in 1889. In the 1920s the company took over a number of iron and steel firms with colliery interests. These included the Carlton Ironworks at East Howle, near Ferryhill, with the linked nearby pit at Mainsforth, which was absorbed in 1923, and

Sir Bernhard Samuelson's East Hedleyhope Pit. Bell Brothers Limited owned Tursdale, Browney and Pagebank, and, in 1906, E. Johnson and Sons had sunk Bowburn Colliery for them, to relieve heavy haulage in the adjoining Tursdale Pit.[47] This, too, was taken over, as was Bolckow, Vaughan and Company Limited, in 1929. The latter had worked pits at Auckland Park, Binchester, Dean and Chapter, Westerton, and a shaft at Merrington Lane, on the site of the old 'Drybread' Ironworks of Messrs Coulson and Company.[48]

Joseph Pease (1799–1872), a Quaker MP, and leading figure in the development of the railways and the port of Middlesbrough had concentrated on coalmining, with his son, Joseph Whitwell Pease, dealing with the ironstone side of the business. In 1898 'Pease and Partners' became a limited liability company, though the interests of the various members of the family, through the generations, became wide and complex. While their operations concentrated on coalmining, they were also involved in ironworks, ironstone mines, cokeworks, chemicals, limestone quarries and wagon building and repair.

By the early twentieth century the Peases operated the great Peases West complex of pits and coke-yards in the Crook–Roddymoor area, and the pits at Waterhouses, Esh Winning and Ushaw Moor. The firm also had a director on the board of T. and R.W. Bower Limited, which owned the Allerton Main Collieries, and, in addition, they operated a pit at Thorne, near Doncaster. Around 1920 Pease and Partners spent £771,233 on sinking down 2,820 ft at Thorne to work the Barnsley and Dunhill seams. At the time this was the deepest shaft in the country, requiring the freezing of the water-bearing strata.[49] When completed, the intended output was to be 1,200,000 tons per annum. W.F. Pease and Arthur Pease also held shares in the Dorman-Long dominated Horden Collieries Limited. By 1939 the Pease and Partners group owned eight collieries employing 4,841 men and producing annually 1,650,000 tons of coal.[50] They also controlled the coal firm of Henry Stobart and Company, and the North Bitchburn Fireclay Company, with Joseph Albert Pease acting as trustee for £287,302 debenture stock in the Weardale Steel, Coal and Coke Company.

Linked to coalmining was their production of coke, undertaken at their Deerness Valley yards and at the great coke oven and by-product works at Bankfoot. J.A. Pease was Chairman of the National Association of Coke and By-product Plant Owners. From their by-product works tar, sulphate of ammonia, and benzole were extracted. The firm owned 52,000 shares in the National Benzole Company Limited and, as chief shareholders, had a director on the board, while they also had a controlling interest in the Power Gas Corporation Limited.[51]

Outside their coal and coke interests, iron manufacture was of great importance. By 1875 J.W. Pease and Partners were the largest workers of ironstone royalties in Cleveland. Sir David Dale, who became manager of Pease's collieries and ironstone mines in 1872, and chairman of Pease and Partners after 1903, was also a director of the Barrow Haematite Steel Company and Consett Iron Company.

The family was also involved in banking. Linked with the bankers Overend and Gurney, the Peases established their own finance house of Messrs J. and J.W. Pease. Due to an inter-family dispute this company later fell into difficulties and ultimately collapsed in 1902, affecting several companies, particularly the North Eastern Railway Company, who held accounts with the bank.[52] Although there were suggestions that the bank should be declared bankrupt, this was never pressed. Quaker colleagues assisted in reducing the debt, and Barclays eventually took over the Peases' bank. By the 1920s, however, the family had members on the boards of Barclays and Lloyds, and had links with the Pearl and the Prudential Assurance Companies.[53]

The Londonderry mining operations at Rainton were closed down in the 1880s, and greater emphasis was placed on Seaham. Further down the coast, a pit was sunk at Dawdon through the limestone and water-feeders by freezing the strata between 1900 and 1908.[54] Another colliery was started at Seaham, 300 yds from the high-water mark, in 1923. The two shafts, the Vane and Tempest, were sunk by the freezing process, to work the Five Quarter seam, at 1,722 ft, and the Busty, at 2,094 ft.[55]

The largest colliery company in County Durham was created by James Joicey, whose father had set up a small mining operation on Tanfield Moor.[56] In 1896 he took over the Earl of Durham's pits, which were then run as the Lambton Collieries Limited. Joicey, who was raised to the peerage in 1906, acquired the Hetton Coal Company five years later. This firm operated the Hetton Lyons, Eppleton and Elemore Pits. In 1920 he added Silksworth Colliery, formerly the property of Lord Londonderry, to his collection. In 1924 these different interests were transformed into a new company, the Lambton, Hetton and Joicey Collieries Limited.

Horden Collieries Limited was set up in 1900 to work around 19,000 acres, including undersea reserves.[57] The initial flotation was undersubscribed because of its highly speculative nature. However, the directors eventually raised the required share capital of £1,500,000, and began sinking the shafts. The mine was of the latest design, and was said to have been used as the model for the reconstruction of the war-damaged French mines. By 1930 Horden Collieries' operations embraced Horden, Blackhall, Shotton and Castle Eden Pits, with a daily output of up to 12,000 tons.

Britain's over-emphasis on mining and heavy industry resulted in serious problems when trade suffered in the face of foreign competition, while other countries' coal industries expanded and a world-wide depression took effect. A short boom had occured in the coal trade, and British industry generally, following the Great War, but the export trade collapsed in the early twenties, and there were major difficulties in the steel industry and shipbuilding. The number of ships built in the north-east fell from 210 in 1920 to 89 in 1923.[58] In the coal industry there were strikes in 1921 and 1926. The latter proved to be a major disaster for the miners, as it was for the trade union movement generally. Hours were increased, with lower wages, which were further affected by the 1928 Plender Award. The stoppage of coal shipments as a result of the 1926 strike also resulted in the expanding Polish coal industry seizing the Scandinavian market, which had previously been largely supplied by Britain.[59]

In Durham the number of people employed in the coal industry fell from 165,246 in 1913 to 128,038 by 1930, and continued to fall, to a level of 98,096 by 1933, at the depth of the depression.[60] Pits were closed or put into mothballs. At Esh Winning 843 men and boys were dispensed with in 1930, and the pit was closed down for twelve years.[61] The colliery was the only major employer in the village. In 1934 there were 228 working pits in Durham, but the number of workers had fallen to 107,873, producing 30,590,000 tons.[62] Taken with Northumberland, the output of the Great Northern Coalfield at that time was 44,421,000 tons. Of this, 12,668,000 tons went for export, principally to western Europe. To maintain production, Durham owners, like those in Northumberland and Scotland, tended to sell their coal at 1/2d. to 1/3d. a ton less than the average UK price, resulting in a loss, in the period 1930–4, of up to 4 1/2d. on the ton.[63] By 1935 some pits were working on a day-to-day basis, while other pits within a group were working alternate weeks. For some collieries this was caused by the failure of Italy to pay for coal supplies it had received and the stopping of further shipments. Washington Glebe Pit, for instance, was owed £20,000.[64] At Holmside and South Moor Collieries it was proposed that the Hedley, William and Louisa Pits should work one week, while the North and South Morrison Pits should work the next.[65] Improvement in the coal industry only came with the re-armament programme. Manpower levels had fluctuated following a slight rise in 1934, and a peak was reached in 1937 of 109,272 workers.[66] Output was also at its highest during this year, 34,538,923 tons, though output per man per shift had fallen from a high of 23.32 cwt in 1935 to 22.82 cwt in 1937, and continued to fall throughout the Second World War. In 1945 output was 18.35 cwt.

At Vesting Day, 1947, when the mines of the country were nationalized, there were 127 collieries left in the county.[67] Throughout western Europe, however, the use of coal as a fuel was on the decline by the 1950s, due to a greater dependence on oil from the Middle East, Nigeria and Venezueala. The higher energy yield from oil compared with that of coal, and the transportation developments in pipe-laying and increased tanker size had a considerable effect on the competitiveness of coal. Refining capacity in the United Kingdom had increased from 3,500,000 tons in 1938 to 20,000,000 tons in 1951.[68] World crude production increased, and by 1958–9 there was a glut of cheap oil on the market, which affected the coal trade, already under increasing threat from other alternative fuels, natural gas and nuclear power.

The National Coal Board consequently planned reorganization and streamlining to improve efficiency and competitiveness, with massive cuts in 'marginal' collieries with low productivity, high costs and declining reserves. The number of collieries in the coalfield had remained fairly stable from 1947 to 1954, but then the number of working pits markedly declined from 133 in the latter year to 34 in 1969.[69] Manpower levels dropped as a consequence. Initially the decline was fairly slow, from 108,291 in 1947 to 100,881 in 1957, before falling steeply to the 1969 level of 34,484. Saleable output actually rose from 24,140,000 tons in 1947 to 27,100,000 in 1951, before the steady decline to 8,384,000 tons in 1977. Of this output, the actual amount produced by the miner in a shift, which had been fairly static from Vesting Day to 1958, ranging from 17.4 to 20.6 cwt, rose steadily to a peak of 35.1 cwt in 1969. Some output was maintained at a limited number of inland sites, but greater emphasis was placed on the coastal pits, with some amalgamation of collieries.

Between 1952 and 1958 a shaft was sunk at Hawthorn as a main drawing-shaft, with new coal preparation and coking facilities, serving the older satellite mines of Murton, Eppleton and Elemore, which were all linked underground.[70] Also in 1958 the NCB began seabed drilling in the North Sea to test the extent of undersea reserves off Blackhall, Horden, Westoe and Wearmouth.[71] These borings established the geological sequence, and identified main coal seams and workable lower seams at the drilling points. These productive units became the main source of mining employment in the county. Plans for increased output for the 1960s in the northern coalfield fell well below the published estimates, and the NCB considered that the most urgent need was for a redeployment of miners to the long-life collieries. Alf Hesler, General Secretary of the Durham Branch of the National Union of Mineworkers, in 1967, spelt out what this meant:

> The price we in Durham must pay is the sacrifice of our traditional mode of life; dwelling in houses clustered around the pit and walking the back lane to the colliery yard. Men must be prepared to go where the work is, to live in one place and travel to another, or to move house and reside in a district where one of the long-life collieries is situated. The alternative is to leave the industry and find other employment.[72]

With the conflict in the Middle East in 1973, and its effects on oil exports, the NCB reduced its colliery closure programme (fifteen during the decade), while increasing investment at the deep mines of the concealed coalfield, with exploration and development work, and increased mechanization, including the installation of rapid-loading systems.[73] Output was mainly taken up by the CEGB, though coke production continued to be concentrated at Derwenthaugh, Fishburn, Hawthorn, Lambton, Monkton and Norwood. In 1979/80 there were nineteen collieries in County Durham, with 23,300 men producing 9,698,730 tonnes of coal, an annual average of 416.2 tonnes output per man.[74] Although British-produced coal had the lowest government subsidy in Europe (£2 in 1981), it still managed to produce the cheapest deep-mined coal, at £34 per tonne. However, during the late 1970s and 1980 British Steel closed its works at Hartlepool and Consett, and agreed to import coking coal from Australia and from Weglokoks, the Polish state coal marketing company. By 1982/3, and the loss of six peripheral

NCB out-to-sea boring tower.

collieries (Eden in 1980, Blackhall and Houghton in 1981, Boldon in 1982, and Marley Hill and East Hetton in 1983), output had fallen to 7,271,811 tonnes, produced by 15,289 men, though on average each man's output had increased to 475.6 tonnes.[75] Following the 1984/5 national strike over pit closures and loss of employment, British Coal (as the NCB became in 1986), cut its remaining outlying operations, and concentrated on the eastern 'super pits' of Dawdon, Easington, Murton, Vane Tempest/Seaham (merged in 1983), Wearmouth and Westoe. In 1986/7 output was gradually rising, with 7,327,564 tonnes being raised by a much smaller workforce of 10,892 men, and productivity having risen dramatically to 664.5 tonnes annual output per man.[76] This had been achieved by mechanical cutting throughout, and power-loading. Output continued to be primarily to the electricity industry. Coke production, however, fell from 930,276 tonnes, made by 1,543 men in 1980/1, to 475,565 tonnes, made by 186 men, in 1986/7. Gas, manufactured at the yards, also fell during this period from 7,982,228 to

Westoe Colliery, 1965. To develop the undersea reserves, a new upcast shaft was sunk, with a tower-mounted multi-rope friction drum winder, the coal being raised in a 15 ton skip.

3,842,673 gigajoules.[77] In 1985 only Fishburn and Monkton Cokeworks remained. In October 1986 Fishburn closed and in 1990 Monkton was shut down.

The decline of the coalfield has continued despite rising productivity and output. Dawdon and Murton closed in 1991. The process is seen as a 'slimming down' of the industry in order to achieve a state where it can appeal to the private sector. This move towards denationalization has been the aim of the Tory government since the declaration made by Cecil Parkinson at the 1988 Conservative Party Conference. If the suggestions made in the N.M. Rothschild study on the industry actually come into effect, there will only be one pit left in Durham at the end of the century, either Westoe or Wearmouth.[78] Increasing emphasis is now placed on opencast coal extraction, either directly by British Coal, or by private firms under licence.[79] The majority of this work is being undertaken in west Durham.

The Durham Miner and his Family

Various factors, including the expansion of coal exploitation, saw the population of County Durham rise from 149,384 people in 1801 to 1,187,361 by 1901. Though there was a rise in each decade, the underlying trend, revealed by the percentage rate of increase over each ten-year period, indicates fluctuations through the century. The population grew until 1841, fell back slightly in the following decade, before rising to a peak during the period 1861–71, after which the growth rate fell noticeably up to the turn of the century and beyond.

The demolition of Ryhope Colliery, following closure in 1966.

The men who dug the coal at the new pits, and who lived in the close-knit colliery rows with their families, were predominantly northerners. The census evidence for the latter half of the nineteenth century indicates that Durham-born people were in the majority in the mining settlements, followed by those born in other northern counties, like Northumberland, Yorkshire, Cumberland and Westmorland. Similar features have been noted in Leicestershire, where the mines were worked primarily by men of that county;[80] and in Glamorgan in the latter half of the nineteenth century native-born people, and those people from neighbouring Welsh counties, formed the greatest mass of the population that worked such coal centres as the Rhondda.[81] Some of the incomers were already experienced miners, like the leadminers who came into the coalfield in 1832.[82] Cumbrians began arriving in the coalfield in the 1820s. Thomas Cowden, of Maryport in Cumberland, wrote in 1822 to a colliery owner: 'Sir we here in this country that you are wanting men and that you will bear the expences Thomas Cowden and my son will go to you.' At the Addison Pit a new miner found starting work hard-going: 'The man we got from Cumberland has hewed 15 tubs today his hands are very sore he says he has only worked 11 days this year. I have let him have some moor money to send for his family.'[83]

Many of the other migrants to the Durham coalfield came from established mining areas, like Yorkshire, Lancashire, Staffordshire, Cornwall and Wales. The appearance of Cornish families in Durham villages is most probably linked to the economic problems in the metaliferous mining industry in Cornwall in the latter half of the nineteenth century. Copper production reached a peak there in 1856, but was seriously affected by foreign competition, chiefly from North and South America, with a slump in 1866. Some miners were absorbed in the tin industry, but many emigrated. The

Women and children at Corey Street, Ryhope.

American Civil War caused a depression in the export trade of the British tin-plate industry, which consequently affected tin mining. Though there was a short boom following the war, the industry returned to depression as a result of competition – in the 1870s from Australia, during the late 1880s from the huge alluvial tin resources of Malaya, and in the 1890s from Bolivian ore. Some miners and their families came to the Durham coalfield, a number in open railway trucks; those coming to work at Wingate Grange in 1866 coming principally from Liskeard and Calstock.[84] Their impact is still recalled in villages such as Murton, by surnames like Treweeke and Pascoe, or by the street names – Truro Avenue, Bude Square and Penryn Avenue.

Some Welsh mining families came from the Welsh language areas of north and west Wales, Y Fro Gymraeg. Elizabeth Mills, who was living at Ushaw Moor Colliery in 1882, could not speak any English.[85] In some Durham villages the Welsh tended to congregate together, like the miners at Whitwell Colliery who lived in 'Welsh Row' at Tudhoe.[86] In 1909 David Lloyd George, then chancellor, paid a visit to the Welsh chapel at nearby Spennymoor .[87]

Outside the mining areas there were other residents in nineteenth-century Durham pit villages who had been born in rural counties like Norfolk, Somerset and Cambridgeshire. The decline in the size of farm labour forces, with increased mechanization, the agricultural depression of the late 1870s, and the comparison of agricultural wages and those available in industry and mining, led farm labourers and their families northward.

The effects of the potato famine on the Irish population, with starvation and typhoid from 1846 to 1851, led many to leave their homeland for America, Canada and England. Probably around three hundred thousand landed in mainland Britain and sought work as labourers and navvies in the factory towns and on the expanding rail network. In the mid-1850s there were 'excavators' from Cavan, Donegal, Monaghan and Antrim laying the main Bishop Auckland to Durham railway line,[88] and they were employed at the collieries and as labourers in the coke-yards. There is some evidence of segregation of Irish families in the iron town of Tow law,[89] and a certain area of housing near the colliery at Esh Winning was known as 'Little Ireland'.[90]

The Irish clearly took some interest in the condition of their homeland, giving money to a relief fund organized at Newhouse Catholic Church in Esh Winning when the potato crop failed in Ireland in 1898.[91] A Durham and Northumberland branch of the United Irish League was established, and meetings attended by up to two thousand Irish, like that in 1904, were held at Wharton Park in Durham City.[92]

There were also city-dwellers, like the Bristol men taken on at Lambton Colliery in 1864/5,[93] or the Londoners who went to work at Pease collieries in the 1870s – 'they are said to be a fine lot, to be "framing" well, and they tell the others, lots more want to come'.[94]

The miner and his family, particularly in the mid-nineteenth century, were highly mobile, moving from one pit village to another as the employment situation merited, with the knowledge that housing or rent was generally provided, and, if it was only a short move, a colliery cart might be provided to transport possessions. Robert Gascoigne is a good example of the wandering miner.[95] He was born at Old Trimdon in 1862, the son of a miner. He started work at Westerton Colliery at the age of twelve, and subsequently found employment, at various times, at Trimdon, Hutton Henry, Craghead, Oxhill, Westwood, Urpeth, Moorsley, Hebburn, Norwood and Greenside. Finally, in 1912 he settled at Dawdon. Up to the age of sixty-four he worked as a hewer, and at the age of seventy-one, in 1934, was still working underground, as a stoneman in the waste.

Employment prospects and working conditions have, at times, also forced the Durham miner to look elsewhere, like those who went to hew coal in Virginia in 1840.[96] In 1879 the Enginemen's Mutual Protection Society established an emigration scheme to assist any of its members who wished to leave Durham for North America or Australia. Several miners and their families left for Illinois and the coalfields of Pennsylvania,[97] or Brisbane in Australia.[98] In 1892 there was a county-wide strike, during which the miners again looked elsewhere. George Hunter, of Johnson County, who kept a close eye on what was happening in the Durham coal trade, offered around $3 a day to fifty miners who would leave, and work longwall in Arkansas.[99] In more recent years, through transfer schemes, miners have moved to other coalfields within Britain.

CHAPTER 2

The Colliery

Colliery Sinking and Plant

Coal was won either by shaft or drift. The drift was more common in the west of Durham, where the seams were nearer the surface. The miners simply dug into a bankside and followed the seam. Elsewhere, seams were worked by shaft, sunk to a depth where it was possible to move into the different levels of coal. In some cases the working seams were linked underground by drift.

Miners at the Thrisleton Flat drift, near Crook, c. 1925.

Once the first turf had been ceremonially cut, the dangerous task of sinking the shaft began. Men had been killed in this work; two died at Littleburn in 1872,[1] and there were some hair-raising incidents. At Silksworth, Andrew Laverick, the chargeman, 'London Harry', and four other men, drilled five holes into white post, a level they had reached in the shaft, in 1872.[2] The engineman had lowered a large metal man-carrying bucket, known as a 'kibble', down to them, and the men placed charges into the shot-holes, and lit the fuses. With so much activity taking place on the surface, the engineman thought he heard a signal, and immediately raised the kibble. The men in the shaft were taken completely by surprise. They pulled at the 'rapper', but the signal wire had snapped. Frantically they tried to cut the burning fuses, but they couldn't stop three of them. Luckily the engineman heard their shouts, and quickly dropped the kibble down to them. They scrambled into it, and had been hauled a few fathoms up the shaft when the charges exploded. Rock flew up past them, but, amazingly, only one of them received a slight cut.

At Whitburn Colliery the sinking was achieved by means of the Kind–Chaudron process.[3] A small trepan, weighing 8 tons, with chisels fitted to its jaws, made the initial bore, 5 ft in diameter. Debris produced in the cutting was taken out with a sludger, and a larger trepan was then lowered into the guiding shaft. This device was twice the weight, and armed with chisel blades of various sizes. Working ten to twelve hours at a time, it cut the shaft to the required size. It was then lined or 'tubbed out', and packed behind with concrete.

Because of water, the sinkers wore waterproofs, backskins and caps with neck-flaps. They were raised and lowered in the kibble, which also took out

Aerial view of Whitburn Colliery, c. 1930.

Sinkers at South Moor, c. 1890.

the spoil; while separate winches raised or lowered the pumps. At Brandon, in 1856, the sinkers were paid 7s. per fathom (6 ft) sunk.[4] The shaft was lined with cast-iron tubbing, concrete and brick. At the 'John' shaft at Hamsterley, in 1908, the technique of 'underhanging tubbing' was used. This involved inserting tubbing segments, and then working below them, with piles driven in, before inserting lower segments.[5]

Water was an almost constant problem in sinking operations, and frequently continued to cause problems during the working life of the colliery. It was diverted or removed by using a variety of techniques ranging from deep sumps to adits, syphons, and centrifugal pumps, consequently forming a sizeable part of the running expenses of a mine.

The most serious difficulties were experienced on the east coast, where shafts were sunk through limestone and underlying sand to the concealed coal-measures. In some shafts the water was extracted by bucket pumping, as was the case at Murton and Blackhall, though this incurred considerable expense with the constant repairing and replacing of the leather buckets. In the most difficult stages of the Blackhall sinking, through the water-bearing limestone, boreholes were drilled, and pure cement pumped into them under high pressure. Once this set, it formed a dam against the water.[6] This cementation process, sometimes known as the 'Bourgii method', was also employed at Horden.

Sinkers wearing waterproofs, at Cockfield or Evenwood.

At Dawdon Colliery the Marchioness of Londonderry cut the first sod of the 'Theresa' shaft, and Viscount Castlereagh the 'Castlereagh' shaft on 26 August 1899.[7] Sinking was carried out with the aid of pumps to a depth of 200 ft in the 'Castlereagh', and 360 ft in the 'Theresa', when the sand deposits and volume of water encountered (7,000 gallons a minute) necessitated a different approach. Freezing was considered the best option, and Messrs Gebhard and Koenig, of Nordhausen in Germany, began work in 1903. Boreholes were sunk around the shaft, and the freezing process commenced by circulating a solution of magnesium chloride, cooled by means of the expansion of liquefied anhydrous ammonia, through freezing tubes. The gaseous ammonia was compressed to about 10 atmospheres per square centimetre, and then liquefied by passing through 2,000 ft of 1 in tube in each cooling tank. This was then taken to refrigerating tanks, where the pressure was reduced, and it was allowed to expand while passing through the coiled tubing in the tanks. The latent heat required to change the ammonia from a liquid to a gaseous state was extracted from brine, which was thereby cooled to the temperature required for freezing the strata. Once frozen, sinking operations continued, and the shafts were lined with cast-iron tubbing in 1906. German contractors also undertook freezing work at Washington Glebe.

The freezing process at Vane Tempest Colliery, 1925.

In 1902, during the freezing of the shaft at Easington (either by a French or a German company, the documentation is unclear) the system failed, and 13,000 gallons of water and sand broke through onto the sinkers.[8] Although the majority of the men escaped, one man was drowned.

While some collieries comprised only one shaft, after 1862 it became law to have at least two. The shaft was circular, of varying size – at Merrington Lane it was 12 ft in diameter, while at Dawdon the completed shaft was 20 ft. 'Braticing' and 'buntings' enabled the shaft to be divided up for raising and lowering cages, their movement controlled by guides or 'skeats' of iron rail. Above the shaft was the towering pit head, with the pulleys by which cages were raised and lowered. The towers were initially of wood, but later of iron and steel, with lattice-work girder construction, and, more recently, the whole tower shrouded in a reinforced concrete casing.

Cage types varied throughout the coalfield, in the number of decks, and the number of tubs each deck could carry. They included double-deckers,

A two-man cage at Burnopfield.

like that at Bearpark, with each deck holding two 5 cwt laden tubs; three- and four-decker cages; and, later, two-decker cages capable of taking ton mining cars. At the 'Theresa' shaft at Dawdon 9 ton capacity skips were used up to the colliery's closure in 1991.[9]

The cages were raised or lowered by means of winding engines, usually erected in tall stone or brick housings. Various types were used in the Durham coalfield. Crowther's vertical single-cylinder lever type was used extensively, for example, at Bearpark and Ryhope.[10] Other forms include single-cylinder horizontal engines, like the J. & G. Joicey engine used at the Annie Pit at Burnhope, and two-cylinder horizontal engines, such as the Varley & Yeadon engine at Thornley, and the Bradley and Craven make at Thrislington. A Robey twin horizontal drop valve type engine was also installed at Wheatley Hill.

During the early decades of the twentieth century there were moves at some new collieries, like Lumley New Winning in 1910, to replace steam-powered winders with electric types.[11] At Medomsley, a Ward-Leonard Ilgner winder was installed in 1914, with DC power.[12] It had 3$^1/_4$ in Lang's lay plough steel winding ropes, with a breaking strain of 40.8 tons, running over 11 ft diameter pulleys. At older collieries electrification involved considerable conversion work. At Ryhope, Fraser and Chalmers of London installed a 500 hp electric winding engine at the West Pit in 1933, and the old overhead gear supporting the pulleys had to be replaced with a lattice-work tower of steel girders.[13]

A Crowther engine, with onsetters and banksmans signals, Ryhope.

A more unusual system was introduced as part of the reconstruction work at Murton following the Great War. A German Koepe winder was installed at the West Pit in 1922, and used an endless rope, which ran from an engine-driven pulley over two headstock wheels, forming a huge loop round a jockey-wheel at the very bottom of the shaft. The cages were hung, and moved, on the vertical ropes of the loop.[14] Following nationalization, the NCB introduced tower-mounted multi-rope friction drum winding engines

The Koepe tower winder house, Murton, 1991.

The multi-rope friction drum winder at Ryhope, 1956.

in the late 1950s at Ryhope, Westoe and Wearmouth.[15] At Dawdon this type of engine was fitted to both shafts, with the Castlereagh engines rating of 750 kW, and the Theresa of 1,500 kW.[16]

Because of the need for steam in the older winding operations, and for use with pumping engines and crab engines, large boilers, usually the Galloway or Lancashire internally-fired type, were set up, with furnaces and chimney. At the new pit at Dawdon, sunk in the first decade of this century, eight Galloway boilers were put into operation, each 30 ft long and 8 ft in diameter, fired by two furnaces, and linked to a 160 ft high chimney.[17] The water tube boiler type, patented by Babcock and Willcox, was used at Thrislington, following surface reconstruction after the 1911 fire.[18] At Murton, water in the Main seam was raised to the surface by means of three 32 in diameter, 60 in stroke Hawthorn-Davey differential pumping engines, with 8 in double-acting rams.[19]

Engine-houses and boilers at Ryhope.

Compressed air power was first used in a colliery at Govan, in Scotland, in 1851, with a beam engine as the compressing engine. Developments were made in Lancashire in the 1860s, and in the 1870s there were trials at Ryhope, using compressed air for underground haulage. At this pit a 32 in bank engine of 150 hp provided the motion for two air-compressing cylinders, made at the Grange Ironworks in Durham City.[20] The air was piped, via four receivers, 4,515 ft down the shaft and along to a double haulage engine. This machine could haul a thirty tub set, each tub carrying 18 cwt, along 3,900 ft of road in seven minutes. Compressed air also came to be used for 'windy picks' and coal cutters, but was, in part, superseded by electricity.

Electricity was first introduced into a British mine at Trafalgar Colliery, Gloucestershire, in 1882. Shortly afterwards, in 1891, an electrical transmission station to power the pumping plant at East Howle Colliery had been established,[21] and by the turn of the century electricity was being extensively used at Durham collieries. Harton and Murton, for instance, had gone all-electric by 1910.[22] The Lady Beatrice, Eppleton and Houghton Pits were using electricity from the motors of Philadelphia power station, near Chester-le-Street, in 1913.[23] By 1929, 155 of the 264 mines in the county had installed electrical equipment.

For miners working underground, away from fresh air, ventilation had to be provided, not only for breathing, but for the removal of gas. Prior to 1862 a number of collieries used only one shaft, for transporting men, hauling coal to the surface, and for ventilation. The fracturing and collapse of the pump-beam into the shaft at New Hartley in Northumberland in 1862 led to

The compressor house at Dawdon Colliery, 1991.

the blockage of the only means of ventilation, resulting in the deaths of 204 men and boys. The resulting inquiry and Act of Parliament made two shafts compulsory in mines – an upcast and downcast shaft, or, in drifts, the drift mouth and an air-shaft. Furnaces were lit at the upcast shaft to draw air through the mine, and trapper-lads tended the doors which controlled and directed the flow of air. Murton, at the turn of the century, used an underground furnace which could circulate 500,000 cubic ft of air a minute through the workings.[24]

From the mid-nineteenth century there was increasing development and use of ventilation by centrifugal fans. An early form was the Guibal type, introduced into Britain in the 1860s, with a 30 to 40 ft diameter wheel, with eight rigid arms fitted with blades. The fan, in its close-housing, drew the air from the mine and forced it out up a curving, *évasée* form of chimney, whose flue widened towards the top. It was first used in the county in an adapted form at Tursdale before becoming more widely used. It was taken up by Straker and Love at Brandon Colliery; by Bolckow, Vaughan and Company to ventilate their Binchester, Westerton and West Auckland mines, and others were used at Washington, Pelton, West Stanley, Oakenshaw, Wingate Grange and Usworth. A modified form was erected at Page Bank.

Waddle-type fans, produced at the Llanelly workshops of Hugh Waddle, were reported to northern mining engineers in 1869. They were used at sites like Brandon, Brancepeth, Wingate Grange, Auckland Park, Beamish, Pelton, Hylton and the Charley Pit at South Moor. Waddles were open-running fans, with the fan and its casing revolving together on the crank shaft of a horizontal engine housed at the side. Air entered a central opening, and was expelled from the tapered end of the fan blades. Other types included Walker fans, constructed in Wigan, which were used at Dean and Chapter

A Waddle fan at Ryhope.

Colliery at Ferryhill [25] and Easington, and the Lemielle fan which ventilated Page Bank Colliery.[26] Improved and faster forms, requiring smaller fans, were introduced, like the Capell, which underwent experimental testing in Sheffield in 1886. It comprised a pierced inner cylinder with wings. The air collected in this chamber was forced at high centrifugal velocity through the holes into an outer chamber, expanding the air. Initially these fans were a single inlet type, but an improved double inlet form was introduced. Examples were used at East Howle and Murton. The high speed Schiele fan was employed at Browney,[27] and the Sirocco at Horden [28] and the Louisa Pit.

Colliery Officials and Safety Men

Overall control of mining operations was generally given to an agent, who was usually an experienced mining engineer. John Buddle was the well-known agent for the 3rd Marquis of Londonderry. The chief agent for the fourth marquis was Vincent Corbett. He was the son of General Sir Stuart Corbett, and was born in Hindustan.[29] After becoming a mining engineer, he worked for a time in Yorkshire before joining Londonderry in 1869. Following the closure of the Rainton Pits, he concentrated on Seaham, greatly developing the pit. Under his direction, the new pit at Dawdon was sunk in 1908, and during his term of office Londonderry collieries achieved an annual output of 1¾ million tons.

The individual collieries were run by managers responsible to the owner or his agent; sometimes a manager might be in control of several operations.

These men were trusted officials, usually over twenty-five years of age, who, in accordance with the changing developments in mining law, had passed an examination, including a viva with a mining board of owners, workers, mining specialists and Mines Inspectors, set up by the Secretary of State. The manager was eventually to hold a ticket proving his competence in all aspects of mining – engineering science, mathematics, geology, use of machinery, theory and practice of ventilation, use of explosives, and general management of the colliery and its workforce.

Colliery managers varied in character. To some, tonnage output was all that mattered. Thomas Robinson, the manager at Ushaw Moor Colliery in the 1880s, ran the mine as he thought fit, fixing good cavils for his cronies, and threatening the eviction of fifty or sixty workers if union representatives who complained about conditions were not removed. William Crawford of the Durham Miners Association (DMA) said that Robinson 'has harrassed our men in the most shameful manner, leaving no device untried for that purpose'.[30] During the Ryhope strike of 1932 the feelings of animosity of the men towards the 'masters' was expressed in this composition:

The Coal Owner's Ten Commandments

1. Thou shall have no other Master but me.
2. Thou shall not make for thyself comforts, nor the likeness of anything to thine own interest, neither on the earth above or the mine beneath. Thou shall have no other Master but me. Thou shall bow down to me and worship me, for I am thy Master, and a jealous Master, and I will show you no mercy but endeavour to make you keep my commandments.
3. Thou shall not take the name of thy Master in vain, lest I sack thee at a minute's notice.
4. Remember that thou work six days with all thy might, with all thy strength, and do all I want of thee, but the seventh day thou shalt stop at home and do no manner of work, but shall do all thou canst to recruit thine exhausted strength for my service on Monday morning.
5. Honour thy Master, his steward, and his deputies, that thy days may be long in the mine down which you work.
6. Thou shall have no unions.
7. Thou shall always speak well of me, though I oppose thee. Thou shall be content if I sometimes find thee work, and pay thee what I think.
8. Thou shalt starve thyself and thy children if it is to my interest.
9. Thou shall have no meetings to consider thy own interests, as I want to keep thee ignorant, and in poverty all the days of thy life.
10. Thou shall not covet thy Master's money, nor his comforts, nor his luxuries, nor anything that is his.[31]

Other colliery managers were severe but fair, maintaining a tight control on the working of the colliery and the village. At Esh Winning the colliery

An overman and pit boys, Ryhope, c.1920.

manager from around 1879 to 1913, J.G. Crofton, would ride on horseback around the colliery streets, and severely reprimand anyone who did not maintain their garden or keep their house tidy. He lived in a colonnaded villa close to the colliery, but looking away from it. The drive to the villa was lined with flower-beds maintained by his gardener. Some managers were popular. When Mr Cruddace, the manager of Philadelphia Colliery, moved to Shincliffe Colliery in 1842, many Philadelphians moved with him.[32]

Below the manager were the 'overmen' who had generally worked up through the ranks to reach this position. Michael Price, who was born at Felling in 1840, recalled that after three years' education, he started as a trapper at South Pelaw at the age of nine, working a fourteen-hour day for 10d. He later became a hand putter, hewer, hewer and stoneman, before becoming a deputy, and, at the age of forty-four, was promoted to overman at Tursdale Colliery.[33] Overmen were appointed to the various shifts as supervisors, with the main aim of ensuring good output. He allocated work, and checked the number of men working in the shift, for work and pay purposes. He checked the work of each man, and on measured-work, the measurements were usually taken on a Thursday, from which wages were calculated.[34] The overman also watched the men into the pit, on to the man-riding sets to the stations, and onto the man-riding belts to the districts. He checked conditions with the deputies, and ensured that materials were made available when required. A report on the mine would be prepared for the manager, and he would also give a report on conditions to the overman of the following shift.

The safe working of the mine was overseen by the deputy overmen, or 'deputies'. They checked the working areas for gas, the supply of air, the condition of the roof and its support, the supply of timber, the state of roadways and machinery, and also undertook shot-firing in their particular area.

The deputy generally entered the working areas first with his safety lamp and checked for the presence of gas, indicated by a 'cap' which appeared over the flame. The supply of air to ventilate and remove gas was checked, and the deputy would put up 'brattacing' to control and direct the air flow through the workings.

He had a simple desk or 'kist', where he recorded the state of his 'district', at different inspections, the information being supplied to the overman or undermanager at the end of his shift. He also noted the names of the workers in the area, on the shift. To help him get round his area, the deputy often used a flat trolley which ran along the tub track.

The deputies also checked that the hewers had not gone beyond their timber, and ensured that they were supplied with what they needed to keep their workplace safe. This included 'props', 'cross-trees', and, if necessary, 'lids' (or 'capping-pieces'). The deputy carried an axe and a saw to cut and prepare this timber. It was also his job to remove redundant timber once coal

Houghton Colliery in 1905.

A deputy at his kist, Greenside Colliery, c. 1930.

extraction in an area had been completed. The roof was first 'jowled' to test if it sounded solid. If it did, the deputy used a maul to knock out the props, before casting them back to be loaded onto a tram. It was the general practice to try and save timber, but, obviously, this was a very dangerous task, and many deputies were killed or seriously injured doing it. John Atkinson, a Government Inspector of Mines, said that fatalities amongst deputy overmen were higher than among the workmen they were there to protect.[35] Developments such as the 'Sylvester' enabled the prop to be hauled out from a safe distance by means of a crank and chain.

Explosives were kept on the surface in a magazine, and when it was needed, the quantity had to be signed for, as the cost was deducted from the miners' wages. Up until 1914 the miner generally fired the shot when he needed it, though at some mines it was only carried out by a person licensed by the manager. At the Brancepeth 'A' Pit, in 1896, it was noted that powder was given out, on application, to the master shifter or the stonemen under his charge, and it was the custom at the colliery for any unused powder to be placed in a canister and taken home until it was required.[36] After 1914 shot-firing became the duty of the deputy, and the explosive had to be carried underground in special canisters.

Setting up pointed rigid steel props, Greenside Colliery, c. 1930.

There were a number of developments in the types of explosives used, the detonators, and the methods of firing. When black powder was used, a hole was drilled and cleaned out, the black-powder would be filled into it, and a 'pricker' inserted. The mouth of the hole would be filled, and the pricker 'stemmed' around with clay. The pricker would then be screwed out, and a 'squib' inserted. The end was lit, and it burnt to a fixed length before shooting into the powder, causing an explosion and bringing down the rock. At Brancepeth 'A' Pit squibs were in use with powder in 1896, in naked light areas. In other parts of the pit the charge was fired by a fuse lit by a wire heated from the flame of a safety lamp.[37] Donald Bain, HM Inspector of Mines, noted that:

> gunpowder and nitro-glycerine compounds have the lowest factor of safety of any explosives in the market, and their use should be prohibited in all dusty and fiery mines, and on all main haulage roads unless they are absolutely wet.

In 1896 a list of approved explosives for use in mines was produced. Later

A deputy with his tools and trolley, Brancepeth 'A' Pit, 1929

developments included detonators fired by battery. There were also particular rules relating to where and when a shot might be fired.

Underground Coal Workers

Underground workers could be generally divided into the coal getters, the haulage workers and those involved in deadwork, though there were numerous jobs included under these broad headings. The grading of work was by

Pneumatic drilling of shot holes in the Stone drift South, Brancepeth 'A' Pit, 1929.

age, strength and experience, from the trapper-lad to the hewer who dug the coal at the face. It was possible for the hewer to ascend the ladder to the ranks of the officials, by study and examination to become a deputy, and even to take a manager's ticket, but for the vast majority there was a lifelong experience of hard labour below and above ground.

Young children starting at the pit were initially given menial tasks, like greasing tub axles, removing tokens, working on the pit heaps, or below ground as trappers. Robert Hall, who was at Philadelphia in 1834, but moved to Shincliffe Colliery at the age of eight, recalled:

> My mother used to carry me on her back to the pit heap, and then I descended the mine to act as a trapper boy. Working hours were very long in those days, extending to 13 hours, and the pay was the miserable sum of ten pence a day.[38]

James Mitchell, reporting on south Durham to the Childrens Employment Commission in 1842, described the trapper's duties:

(opposite) Setting up a hand drill stand, Axwell Park, 1930.

> He sits himself in a little hole, about the size of a common fireplace, and with the string in his hand : and all his work is to pull that string when he has to open the door, and when man or boy has passed

Men and a pit boy in the Ballarat seam, Brancepeth 'A' Pit, 1929.

> through, then to allow the door to shut of itself. Here it is his duty to sit, and be attentive, and pull his string promptly as anyone approaches. He may not stir above a dozen steps with safety from his charge, lest he should be found neglecting his duty, and suffer for the same.[39]

Sitting in total darkness for hours, there was the great danger that he might fall asleep; if he did, he would get a prod (at least) from the deputy's yard-stick, or be whipped by the pony drivers who were trying to get through the door. Trapping was an initiation to underground work and conditions, the darkness, and the creaking of timbers.

Septimus Martin, of East Herrington, wrote, in about 1918, of his anxiety at starting work in the pit:

> Before November was out I was informed to see the surface keeker who gave me a note for an oil safety lamp, also a note for the store-keeper for a thong of pigskin to be made into a whiplash, to be secured upon a short shank, finally my mother purchased a pint tin bottle for water, made by the local tinker. Suddenly I was disturbed by someone shaking me and saying 'Time to get up, Time to get up', but to me it seemed unreal in the middle of the night to be wakened from sleep, when I did get roused I found out that it was my mother still saying 'Time to get up, come along little feller, time to get up'. Then I asked what time it was, and my mother said it was quarter to three, so I got out of bed and was soon downstairs sitting by a warm fire and putting

(opposite) Four pit lads at Shotton Colliery.

> my clothes on for the first time as a real underground miner. . . . Then my mother filled my new tin bottle with cold water from the tap, then making a few sandwiches of bread and jam . . . my mother said to me 'Good morning son and be careful'. 'I was literally scared of going down the mine, even the action of getting into the mine cage with such a small winding rope filled me with fear.[40]

As boys grew older and stronger they became haulage workers. 'Pony-drivers', usually fourteen or fifteen years of age, were employed to take a number of tubs, a 'set', from a 'flat' to the 'landing' or drift mouth, where they were taken out by rope haulage. It was generally the wagonwayman who taught the boy how to handle the pony, and more experienced boys also provided guidance.

Horseroads were generally fairly dangerous places. In 1924, for instance, there were eleven deaths and 3,394 injuries on these roads, in the county.[41] One example occured at Houghton Colliery on the 3 December 1929:

> Two driver boys were proceeding out-by with full tubs when the second tub got off the way. After looseing and driving the pony a yard or two away the boys began to lift the tub onto the way, one boy held the tub whilst the other was pushing it onto the rails. At this moment a fall of stone occured and practically covered Peter Bent, of Newtown, the boy who was placing the tub on the rails. The other boy went for assistance, and returned with Thomas Race, to find Bent completely buried, with the exception of his head and shoulders. The boy called to Race, 'Get me out', but Race could not do so because of the small stone which was falling from the roof. The place was illuminated by the light of only a single lamp.
>
> Sending the other boy for assistance, Race courageously lay with his body over Bent's head and shoulders, and allowed the stone to fall over him. After Race and the boy had been released there was a large fall of stone. Happily, with the exception of shock they escaped without any ill effects.[42]

Around sixteen, as a boy became stronger, he moved on to 'putting'. Putters supplied the face-workers with empty ('chum') tubs, and removed full tubs to a flat. They also undertook additional tasks, such as taking in timber, and dealing with the tub loads of clay, water, lime, bricks, rails etc., for which there were established additional rates of pay. This work was either done by hand or with the aid of a pony. There were different terms for the hand putters, depending on their physical strength. A putter who did not have the strength to push tubs alone was known as a 'headsman', and was assisted by another boy, known as a 'foal' if he was younger. Those of equal age were called 'half marrows'. Even the older putters needed assistance on some gradients, and a 'helper-upper' would be called for, although he could only assist if the slope was greater than that fixed by agreement between the

(opposite) Putting a tub back on the rails, Axwell Park, 1930.

A pony putter at Greenside Colliery, c. 1930.

union and management. To light their way, in naked light pits the putter fixed a candle to the tub he was pushing, while in gassy pits, the putter carried a safety lamp, weighing three to four pounds, hung around his neck on a leather thong. Obviously, he had to be careful that the lamp did not swing and hit the tub.

A twenty-year-old hand putter at Croxdale Colliery recalled the pushing of a full tub, containing from 6 to 9 cwt, through the low workings, and described it as 'slavery'.[43] In a 2 ft 8 in seam he remembered, in particular, how his bent back scrubbed the roof, knocking off the scabs over his spine, making them bleed, and how the wet, cold canvas ventilator flaps invariably scraped the sores.

Putters were paid by the score of full tubs brought out, which could be from twenty to twenty-five tubs, each tub marked by the putter's token. He would bring in a bunch, normally attached to his belt, and hang them up on a nail near his work-place ready for use. The putters also received a payment related to the distance they had to travel in supplying the hewers with tubs. A set starting distance was known as a 'rank' or 'renk' of 80 yd, for which a

Two pony-putters, one with a whip, at Ryhope.

particular amount would be paid. In the 1870s the rank was around 1s. 4d., and a penny per score for every 20 yd beyond the rank. Their allocation to particular hewers was decided, like the hewer's position at the face, by 'cavilling'.

The change from putter to 'hewer' was not always instant, but often involved a gradual acquisition of experience of the new task – from hewing but concentrating on putting, to become a 'hewing putter', and ultimately a hewer. Some men continued as putters, and in 1918 it was agreed that a putter who was over twenty-one was considered as equal to a hewer with regard to housing, rent and coal allowances, and the minimum wage.

The hewers were the coal winners, and were usually over twenty-one years of age. It was their job to produce good round merchantable coal, and they were paid on piece-work with some allowances for conditions. Two methods of working were used – 'bord and pillar', and 'longwall'. In bord and pillar, two main 'winning headings' were cut from the shaft to form a 'district'; this work normally being done by 'bargain-men', who had negotiated a price with the management. Parallel bordways were then driven, at right angles to the 'cleat' of the coal, followed by narrower roads cut at ninety degrees, known as 'headways' or 'walls'. This criss-cross pattern created pillars of coal of a determined size, which were temporarily retained to support the roof. This extractive process was known as 'working the whole'. Once this had been completed, the pillars could then be reduced, either by 'fast jenkin', cutting into and through a pillar, or by piecemeal slicing off from the side of the pillar, initially by 'skirting', and then by lifting off individual 'juds' of coal, in what became known as the 'broken mine'. The area cleared of coal pillars was called the 'goaf', and the roof would be allowed to sink.

A hewer at Brancepeth 'A' Pit.

In longwall, coal pillars were not retained, the system aiming at complete extraction in one process by cutting from a long face. This was done by working with either advancing or, less commonly, retreating faces. In the first, a main roadway or gate, the 'mothergate', and a series of parallel working gates were worked forward, at a safe distance from the shaft. The coal was then cut from the sides of the roads in long faces, and the roof subsequently supported by pack walls of debris.

With the retreating method, the roads are driven to a boundary, and linked at ninety degrees to create a working face, which could then be cut back towards the shaft.

In the extraction process the seam was undercut, or 'kirved', and the edges 'nicked' vertically. Pressure then weakened the position of the kirved coal, and it would then be brought down by the hewer 'ripping' it with his pick. Sometimes the coal might be supported by chocks (or 'sprags') until it was ready to be brought down. In hard coal a shot might be needed. The coal was then filled into tubs by the hewer using a broad-bladed shovel. Frequently this work had to be done by the miner kneeling or even lying on his side and sometimes a wooden 'cracket' would be used to give the hewer some support.

To ensure the safety of the hewer, the deputy supplied him with timber to secure his work-place. The deputy would put up the initial supports at the start of the shift, but the hewer normally did any other necessary timbering as his work progressed. The deputy would, however, check the hewer's timbering during a later inspection. Initially props were of timber, but later rigid metal types were introduced and, ultimately, in the modern pits, hydraulic power supports. In roadways timbering, and later, arched girders, were erected at fixed distances.

Jack Nicholson, sitting on a cracket, hewing in the Brockwell seam, Brancepeth 'A' Pit, 1929.

A hewer at Axwell Park, 1930.

Deadwork was normally undertaken during the night shift (around 8 p.m. to 4 a.m. in the three-shift system) and was organized by a 'master shifter'. Basically this shift prepared the workings for the fore-shift coming in – by undertaking stonework and repairs. In longwall, for instance, once the coal in a particular section had been extracted, the stone left below it – the 'canch' – had to be removed. A hole would be cut into the rock face by a 'driller', about 6 in from the floor, and might be plugged with wood and left until it was ready to be fired. When the time came, the stone would be detonated, and then a 'stoneman' would come and clear the debris, a job sometimes referred to as 'ploating the canch', and pack it in the side wing which had previously been cleared. A pack wall would initially be constructed in this wing, with a gap between it and the coal ahead, before the rest of the stone was 'stowed'. The gap and pack wall ensured that when the coal in front was extracted, it could be kept clear and clean of the stowed stone. Excess stone which could not be effectively stowed, had to be taken out. In addition, it was necesary to make height, to allow the passage of tubs, and the top canch stone had to be brought down.

The hewer was paid by the number of tubs filled, tub size ranging from 8 to 10 cwt, each tub being marked by the hewer's token, secured to a nail inside. Score price varied according to selling price, and if a tub did not contain the required amount, no payment would be made on that tub. Excessive amounts of stone mixed with the coal could also lead to a fine, and the tub would be set out, the token indicating the hewer responsible. The hewer's wage was also affected by the different conditions and aspects of the job, and the monies paid out were also dependent on local and county agreements. Working the broken, for instance, meant a lower payment than working the whole. Geological conditions – the height of the seam, the presence of faults, hitches and rolls, and water – also influenced the wage, as did the amount of clay and 'ramble' that had to be moved.

Allowances were made for travelling time. As the face increasingly became further from the shaft bottom, so the miner had longer to walk before he even started work – sometimes 2 or 3 miles. After walking for such a distance, often carrying equipment, the miner was not in the best condition for starting an arduous day's work. To transport the men to the face, collieries began using empty sets of tubs on rope haulage, known as 'man-riding' sets. There were occasional accidents with these sets. At Greenside, in 1927, eighty men in the foreshift were travelling inbye when the pin linking the tail-rope to the set became detached. The set ran out of control, and nine men jumped out and were injured. The remainder stayed in the tubs and escaped when the set stopped at a rise.[44] In 1919 man-riding cars were introduced at Horden Colliery. In 1932 trains, operated by wire rope and a stationary engine driven by compressed air, were installed in the Hutton seam at Dawdon, saving the miners the 3 mile walk to the undersea face.[45] The system had two trains, one travelling in, while the other was hauled out. Each train was made up of twenty-two cars, capable of carrying a total of 132 men. Within thirteen minutes the train reached the terminus, 1½ miles in. The men then transferred to man-riding sets, which took them to the face. Belt conveyors were also used for man-riding, but trains are now common, either battery powered or diesel.

An underground train at Easington, 1954.

Due to the unavoidable natural conditions in certain areas of the workings, certain inequalities in working would arise, and thus an attempt to equal out the difficult and easier workings among the men was made by cavilling. This was a system of drawing lots for work places each quarter, and at most collieries there were established rules on the subject. The system resulted in rotation so that when men were cavilled inbye and outbye side of a flat, the first cavil on the outbye side would be the first to move inbye side, and the last cavil on the inbye side would be the first to move outbye side. The putters supplying the different hewers with tubs were consequently affected in the number of tubs they moved by the same conditions that affected the hewers' output. They were, therefore, subject to cavilling, varying the distance of putting, but rotating so that things were equalized.

In the shift system it was common for two hewers to marrow themselves together to work an area or stall, from which they shared the going rate of pay. This system developed a close friendship between miners who shared out the work. Prior to 1910 fore- and back-shifts were worked, with a shift of putters and datal workers, but with the eight-hour legislation, a night shift was introduced. There were variations in hours from pit to pit, but the three shifts were approximately 4 a.m. to 11 a.m., 9 a.m. to 4 p.m. and 3 p.m. to 9 p.m., with two shifts of putters from 6 a.m. to 2 p.m. and 1 p.m. to 9 p.m.

From the miner's actual wage the hewer had to provide his own drill and pick, usually bought at the Co-op store, and a deduction would be made for pick-sharpening. If he needed a shot firing, the cost of powder was also deducted from his wage, as was money for health and recreation schemes,

Miners with 'midgy' lamps, Gordon House Colliery.

and the aged miners' homes. The owners, for their part, provided housing or rent, and at the pit they allocated shovels, mauls, wedges, besoms, safety lamps and tokens to the workers.

Where seams were not gassy, candles in home-made holders were spiked to pit props, while small, open, 'midgy' fuel lamps, and carbide lamps, were used. In gassy pits safety lamps were used. These were oil or spirit fuel lamps, lit on the surface, and locked, either magnetically or with a rivet, before they were taken into the mine. It was common practice to blow on the lamp before it was taken down, and the deputy would blow on it again to check it before the miner went to his work place. If the lamp flame did go out, some pits had a special container into which the lamp could be placed and re-lit, though it only tended to work if the lamp was still warm. These devices had to be placed well away from the working areas, and not in a return airway. More often than not the lamp, in the interests of safety, had to be taken to the surface and re-lit. Some collieries employed a boy, known as a 'lamp-carrier', who would take lamps out to the lamp cabin, have them re-lit, and bring them back to the workers.

Miners with flame safety lamps at Wooley Colliery, c. 1920.

A number of lamp types might be used in a mine, deputies' and officials' lamps often being different, particularly those for gas testing. Of the safety lamps, the Davy lamp was invented around 1816, and comprised an oil reservoir, with a burner encased within wire gauze which cooled the flame. The gauze, however, affected the light quality, and the flame could blow out in air currents of a certain level, or even be carried through the gauze. Richard Heckles, the chief viewer at Houghton Colliery, modified the Davy by placing it into a container, which became known as the 'tin can Davy'.[46] It was used at Usworth in 1886, and by officials at Wingate Grange in 1906. A Davy lamp with a sliding shield was in use at Trimdon Grange in 1882. The Geordie used both a glass cylinder and an outer gauze cylinder around the flame, which received air via holes in the lamp rim.

The Clanny lamp replaced the lower gauze of the Davy lamp with a glass surround to improve the light level, with the later addition of a bonnet to prevent air sending the flame through the gauze. The Clanny was used at Seaham in 1880, and both the Davy and Clanny types were still in use at Washington Glebe in 1908.

The main developments from the Clanny were the Mueseler and Marsaut lamps. The Mueseler had an inner cylinder set over the flame, enabling the products of combustion to pass up and out under the bonnet, while fresh air could enter the outer chamber and feed the flame. The Marsaut lamp, on the other hand, had two separated layers of gauze, and was used at the coalface at Wingate in 1906, along with Donald lamps, locked with a lead plug.

Ackroyd and Best lamps, made at Morley, near Leeds, used a mineral oil fuel, and were used at Lumley, Lambton, New Herrington, Kimblesworth and Houghton Collieries in 1913. Protector lamps of the Protector Lamp & Lighting Company of Eccles, which had a lockable oil spout on the side, were also used. Later versions of this lamp could be lit electrically. Patterson flame lamps were also used from the first half of this century, including re-lighter lamps.

In the late nineteenth century electric lamps began to be manufactured. Miners were initially unwilling to use them because of their extra weight, and, unlike flame safety lamp, they did not reveal the presence of gas. However, they were safer to use, and were gradually accepted. Murton Colliery introduced Sussman electric lamps in 1897, as a trial, and by late 1899 had acquired 1,000 of them.[47] The gradual increase in the number of electric lamps nationally is apparent around the beginning of the Great War. In 1914 there were 679,572 flame safety lamps and 75,707 electric lamps, but by 1915 there were 610,088 flame safety lamps and 95,167 electric lamps in use in Britain. In the northern coalfield the number of electric lamps had increased during that time from 6,978 to 7,152. Nationally the principal electric types were the Ceag and Oldham lamps. By 1929 the proportions had changed, with 401,510 flame and 383,333 electric lamps.

The Oldham lamp comprised a casing containing a two-volt battery with a cap and glass cylinder around the bulb. It was in use at Axwell Park in 1930, while the Wolf, which was powered by a nickel-cadmium battery, had an

Men with electric hand lamps, Axwell Park, 1930.

ebonite bulb over the light bulb. Because of their shape, these lamp types were sometimes nicknamed 'lighthouses'.

Electric cap lamps were in use in the coalfield certainly by the 1920s. They included the Ceag; the Edison model 'J' cap lamp which was worn by deputies at Murton in 1942; the Oldham 'G W' cap lamps worn by miners at Eppleton in 1951; and Patterson SS.1s used at Horden in 1953. There was considerable opposition to a lighting regulation which came into force in 1939 which required high power flame lamps to be used as the only form of lighting by all workers. Men working in bords and headings on their own were to have one with them, while in longwall faces one person in eight must have one, to check for gas. The principal objection to reverting to the flame lamp was that the cap lamp gave a clearer light than the flame lamp, which had to be kept at a safe distance when swinging tools; it gave off a direct beam, which made checking the condition of the roof easier, and it did not flicker like the flame lamp, which could result in nystagmus. W. Stones of Morrison Busty lodge considered that if deputies were confined purely to safety work, including increased gas testing, it would remove the necessity of having to use the flame safety lamps, and the miner could rely on the cap lamp.[48]

Electric lighting was in use at some pits by the 1890s, though at that time it was confined to the area around the shaft, in a main airway. The 'Arc' incandescent lamp was in use above and below ground at Elemore by 1894.[49]

The use of compressed air below ground made it possible for the hewer to use the pneumatic or windy pick. Compressors and storage tanks were normally set up on the surface, and the compressed air was taken by pipe down the shaft to the workings. The hewer then connected his pneumatic pick to the pipe by means of a tube known as a hogger. These hewers were sometimes known as 'pickmen', and they marrowed themselves together to pool their earnings. They were responsible for the picks, and either bought the oil for it, or were supplied with a small flagon by the management. Two types of pick point were used, one for coal and another for stone. The points were numbered, and could be sent out for sharpening and then returned to the correct pickman. Their wage included allowances for oiling the pick, and coupling and uncoupling the hoses at the air mains. Once the pickman finished his shift, he handed the pick over to his marrow, or stored it in a kist that was provided.

While the pneumatic pick was supposed to cut coal cleaner than a cutter, it tended to produce a lot of dust, and in a confined space the miner was constantly inhaling this dust. In August 1935 there was a dispute at Beamish Mary Colliery when 186 of the 205 facemen refused to use pneumatic picks, the men stating that they were impossible to use without great difficulty, and were a danger to their health.[50] The men were given their notices, but eventually agreed to use the picks, and the strike terminated in November.

Mechanical means of working coal were being used in the county in the late nineteenth century. The Haswell Mechanical Coal-getter, used at that colliery in 1883 to work hard steam coal, generated bursting force by combining a screw, lever and wedge,[51] but competition from American machine-cut coal stimulated the development of underground cutters and loaders in Britain, particularly from around 1902. At the Margaret Pit of Newbottle

Mr Ramshaw using a pneumatic pick in the Jet seam, Brancepeth 'A' Pit.

Collieries, an electric generating plant was erected in 1891, and by 1902 it supplied the power for three 6 ft 4 in diameter disc cutters, of diamond type, which were used in the longwall faces of the Brass Thill.[52]

By the end of 1905, seventy-three coal-cutters were in use in the county, forty-two powered by electricity, and thirty-one by compressed air.[53] At the Lady Beatrice Pit, New Herrington, disc, bar, 'Champion' and the Sheffield-made percussion 'Little Hardy' coal-cutters were tried, but by 1913 they had all been removed, and the pit had gone back to manual coal working.[54] This regression had also occurred at the North Biddick (Botany Bay) Pit near Harraton, around the same time.

At Seaham a 'pom pom' cutter was used. This machine used varying sized rods fitted with multi-bladed pick heads, seemingly to undercut coal using compressed air power. Their productivity was low compared with coal cut by pick.

The principal form of coal-cutter used was the undercut type, comprising a driving unit, haulage unit, and gearhead, with a cutter chain on a jib. Once set up on the floor, 'jibbing-in' brought the cutter blade into the face. An anchor prop was then set up at a fixed distance along the proposed cutting track, and a haulage rope was stretched out from the machine and attached to the prop. The cutterman then set the machine cutting along the face. As it progressed, an assistant cleared the kirved coal, and supported the seam with sprags. Once the machine reached the anchor prop, it was reset, and the process was repeated until the length of the face had been kirved. The remainder of the coal was then cut down by the hewer's pick. In the 1930s Easington was using Anderson Boyes air-driven arc wall chain type coal-cutters, fixed to a bogey and running on rails.[55] With this system the machine was easily directed to the face, and the jib literally cut in an arc. Horden Colliery, around this time, operated caterpillar-mounted arc-shearing machines.

During the Second World War American machines were introduced into Durham collieries under Lend Lease. At Eppleton, short wall coal-cutters were introduced – a type capable of cutting an area of between 12 and 30 in in width, while hauling itself sideways along a rope. Following nationalization drum-shearers were used at Blackhall, and in the High Main at Dawdon, prior to its closure in 1991.[56] At the latter pit, a Canadian Dosco roadheading machine was used for development work.

Various separate systems were developed for loading the cut coal. Compressed air-powered shovels were, for instance, used at Easington and Waterhouses, the blade flipping the coal back into a tub. Duckbill loaders were introduced for use in bord and wall work, and comprised a shovel and shovel trough linked to a telescopic shaker conveyor. The shovel could be swivelled through a wide arc to clear up the coal, and the digging motion was produced by the shaker. Duckbills were used at Eppleton, and at Easington in 1951, where the district in which they worked was known locally as 'The Duckbill'.

By 1945 Joy loaders and shuttle cars were in use at Eppleton.[57] The Type 12 BV loader used at this colliery was mounted on caterpillar tracks, and its gathering arms collected loose coal at the face, directing it, via a scraper conveyor, to a back unit which discharged the coal to 3-ton capacity, battery-powered, shuttle cars. These cars then took the mineral to a belt conveyor.

In 1930 machines which both cut and loaded coal began to be developed in Britain, in particular the Anderson Boyes Company's Meco-Moore cutter-loader. This make was installed at Boldon Colliery in 1940.[58] German compressed air coal ploughs were introduced at Morrison Colliery around 1947, working in the Bottom Busty. Cutter ploughs and the Rapid Plough were also introduced into the coalfield, and for the thin seams of western Durham, the Gusto Multi-plough was used in 1954 at Waterhouses.[59] This was the first pit in Britain to use such a machine. It comprised an armoured scraper chain conveyor with a number of small ploughs running backwards and forwards along the face side of the conveyor. It worked in 18 in seams, and cut and loaded a 3 in strip of coal each journey. The Huwood slicer, used at Easington in 1954, was a multi-bladed plough, with an armoured conveyor. Subsequently, multi-jib cutter-loaders were used at Bearpark, and other power-loading systems were introduced at East Hetton, Eppleton, Herrington, Houghton, Wearmouth and Westoe.

The mechanization of the process of taking out the cut coal from the face was achieved, with varying degrees of success, by the use of belt conveyors. In 1903 Blackett's patent conveyors were introduced, and by 1913 these were being used on longwall faces at Chopwell and Kimblesworth.[60] Between 1948 and 1953 the use of belts more than doubled in Durham, with the total belt length in the county rising from 74.6 miles to 175.1 miles.[61] By 1953, of the ninety-five collieries in the Durham division of the NCB,

A Huwood slicer, Easington, 1954.

A scraper-conveyor, Greenside Colliery, c. 1930.

ninety-four had gate conveyors – the main belt transporting coal to a loading point or to a trunk belt – although, at that time, only fifty-two of the collieries possessed trunk conveyors .[62] Dust tended to be a problem, and sprinkler systems were needed to suppress it. Even so, there were occasional fires – fourteen are recorded in the county from 1940 to 1953. It was also possible to create loading points, where the conveyor end was raised above the road, and where the coal could be filled into tubs, and transferred to the shaft.

In the days before this level of mechanization had entered the pits, the coal, cut and loaded into tubs at the face by the hewer, was taken out by the putter to a flat. From here, a pony-driver would couple two or three tubs up to the limbers of a pony and transport them to a landing. Often there were several landings and a main landing, commonly known as the 'big landing'. This was the organizing and transport centre for coal on its way to the shaft, and for empty tubs coming back in. Tubs would be coupled into sets of around twenty or thirty tubs by landing lads, and hauled out by a wire rope to the cage. Two systems of rope haulage were used in Durham – 'main and tail' and 'endless rope'. With main and tail, an engine with two drums was used, with full and chum tubs using the same track, the main rope running on rollers down the centre of the track to wheels inbye, and the tail rope running on guides at the road's edge. The main rope was attached at the front of the set, and the tail rope (which was slightly thinner) at the end of the set, and a signal sent to the engineman. The engine was then set in motion, and the main rope pulled the set out, wrapping around its drum, while the tail rope ran through loose, and

A loading point on a wagonway, Greenside Colliery, c. 1930.

A loading point in the Hutton seam, Easington, 1954.

Rope haulage at Brancepeth 'A' Pit, 1929.

around an inner pulley. When the chum tubs, as a set, were ready to go inbye, the tail rope was attached to the front, and the main rope to the back, and the set was hauled by the engine, with the tail rope pulling. An 'offtakes man' changed the ropes on sets moving to or from branch roads.

In the endless rope system, two tracks were needed, the tub being clipped onto the rope and hauled in or out. The technique was in use at Axwell Park in 1900, where 11,000 ft of crucible steel wire rope, weighing 6 tons, was installed.[63] Haulage, by steam engine, moved around 1,800 tubs per day. Pelton Colliery used a similar system.[64]

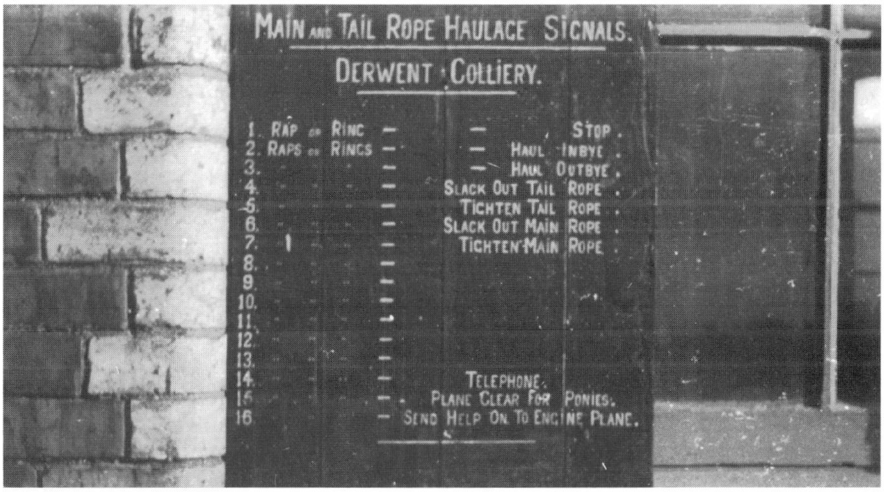

Rope haulage signals at Derwent Colliery.

An onsetter at Burnopfield.

The 'wagonwayman' was responsible for the haulage roads, and for the movement of sets to and from the landings. Because of the speed at which sets were moved along haulage roads, refuge holes were provided in the sides of the workings at regular intervals.

At the bottom of the shaft, an 'onsetter' (sometimes known as a 'waiter on') was responsible for seeing the men and boys safely into the cage at winding time. Once in, he secured the gates and 'rapped' to the banksman and the winding-engineman.

Surface Operations

The engineman sat in the enginehouse at bank, and was highly skilled in the raising and lowering of the cage. He worked in comparative isolation, to avoid distraction, and only authorized persons like the manager, under-manager, engineer, foreman-smith and electrician were allowed in the enginehouse. For obvious reasons he was not allowed to leave the controls when men were entering or leaving the cage, or when the shaftsmen were at work. When the cage was carrying tubs it would be raised at around 24 ft per second, while men travelled at half that speed.

(opposite) An offtakes man at Brancepeth 'A' Pit, 1929.

In front of the engineman would be a marked depth indicator, and dials and bells used when the banksman and the onsetter signalled him. There were some variations in signals. When men were about to enter the cage to ascend, the onsetter might rap three times to the banksman and engineman, and when they were ready to ascend, the signal would be one rap. For descending, the banksman rapped three times to the onsetter and the engineman that the men were about to enter the cage, then two raps to tell the engineman that they were ready to travel. The onsetter then rapped once to the engineman and the banksman. There were also various raps for different seams, and for signalling when raising or lowering tubs.

When a cage was being raised to the surface, it knocked up metal 'keps', which then flipped back as it passed, and formed holding supports for the cage as the men were released and the tubs unloaded. A banksman opened the cage gates, and took the men's tokens. These were then taken to the lamp cabin, where the miner collected one from a board, along with his lamp, at the beginning of a shift. The tokens were a guide to the number of men actually down the mine, in case there was an explosion or other serious

Interior of the winding-engine-house, Brandon 'C' Pit, 1929.

accident.

The 'heapstead' was the focal point of the surface processing of coal, and, of necessity, the structure was heavily constructed, often with steel flooring, to withstand the regular movement of laden coal tubs.

The tubs were removed from the cage either manually, or by ram, and weighed. They were also examined by the bank inspector or 'keeker', and those containing excessive amounts of stone would be laid out, and the miner could be fined. As a check on the amount of coal raised, from which the wage was computed, the owners employed a weighman, usually known as the 'master's weighman'. The workers, fearing that this appointment could be used to fraudulently alter the weights in favour of the management, paid for a man to check the weights. The 1887 Coal Mines Regulation Act made it possible to have these 'checkweighers' – men trusted by the men, and victors of a works ballot – to check the weight.

The banksmen then undertook the heavy task of pushing the tubs into metal holding-frames called 'kick-ups', which were tipped, casting the coal down onto the screens. Once emptied, the frame was hauled back, the tub discharged, and the hewer's and putter's tokens collected by a 'token-boy', who hung them on a nail on a board in the token cabin, so that the output of each worker could be ascertained. The information was collected daily, and at the end of a fortnight the pay bill would be produced, based on the total

Kick-ups at Blackhall Colliery, 1929.

Tubs and creepers at Easington, 1954.

number of tokens belonging to each worker. The tubs, meanwhile, were ready to be returned to the pit. Another type of turning frame was the automatic rotary tippler. In some collieries, like East Hetton, much of this process was being mechanized by the end of the nineteenth century.[65] Full tubs ran down inclined surfaces from the cage to self-righting kick-ups, and, once emptied and levelled, were discharged by an incoming full tub. The empty tubs were then taken by endless belt to sidings ready for the cage to take them back below ground. This process could be carried out by four boys. At Hylton, and elsewhere, 'creepers' were used to raise the tubs back up to the shaft, where they were placed into the cages by the banksmen.[66]

The screens were generally covered, though those at Twizell Pit had only a flimsy canvas sheet over the work area, which made the screening particularly uncomfortable in bad weather.[67] The covered screens were generally illuminated by a lamp, lit by the keeker, who was in charge of bank operations. Prior to mechanization two men generally worked at each screen, dragging the coal over it. By 1901 Bearpark, for instance, used a travelling scraper to carry the coal over the screens onto the picking belt.[68] Later, 'jigging screens' were used to sort and size grade the coal. Grades included 'bests', 'nuts' and 'smalls'.

Old or disabled miners and young boys, called 'wailors', were employed in basic cleaning, picking out shale and band, as the coal was run down from the screen. John Green described his work at Black Boy Colliery in 1842, when he was eleven:

I have worked three years at the top of the bank. When I went first on

The picking-belt at Easington, 1954.

the bank I wailed the coals – that is, picked the stones out. I got 9d. a day. I came to bank at three in the morning, summer and winter. I threw the stones into a heap: people come and put them into tubs, and they are rolled away and thrown down the side of the bank. I got coffee before I came to work, and bread; sometimes there was butter on the bread. I began work at three, and worked till six; then I took some coffee and bread, which I had fetched from home, and kept under the screens. The wailors stand about the waggon, and when the coals roll down the screen into the waggon, they see the stones and pick them out. . . We see by the light of a great fire which is kept in a lamp, which hangs on a chain from the top of the screen. After coffee and bread I had to come back and pick stones again till 11; when it was one I had cheese and bread, and water if I liked. I rested a quarter of an hour to take the bread and cheese; after having bread and cheese I went to pick stones again, and worked till five at night. . . I never get thumped on the bank; I like it nicely.[69]

Picking was increasingly done from endless belts. At New Brancepeth belt boys were paid piece-rates of 0.253 to 0.352d. per box filled with debris in 1909, the boys on each belt sharing their earnings.[70]

Heavy horses used for shunting, Harton Colliery, c. 1890.

The coal, processed at the screens, fell into hoppers which, in turn, fed the coal down into waiting trucks. The early trucks were wooden chaldrons known as 'black wagons', which were later increased in size. These later changed into the more familiar coal truck, with a wooden body, and the developed metal body. Coal trucks were made at Motherwell, by Hurst, Nelson and Company, and at Wakefield by Charles Roberts and Company. Heavy horses were sometimes used for shunting, but many mineral lines in the county used 'tanky' engines to transfer coal from the pit down line to the sidings for transfer to a main track. A series of incline systems were also set up in the county, like the Wooley and Stanley inclines linking the Mary Pit at Waterhouses to Bankfoot at Crook,[71] or the Garesfield incline.[72]

Waste which was not stowed, either as a pack or in the goaf, had to be brought to the surface and tipped. This could either be done at a drift, by extending tub line away from the entrance, and tipping; or by erecting a gantry from the heapstead to a suitable site. Care was needed in the construction of such heaps because of the danger of slippage. At the coastal pits

Horden Colliery, hoppers, trucks and 'Horden' tank engine, 1937.

aerial flights were erected to dispose of the waste at sea. Land tips often contained some amount of coal, and during industrial disputes strikers resorted to the heaps for fire coal. Sadly, in several cases men died burrowing into the heaps. Some reprocessing of tips has been undertaken to recover coal.

From the very late nineteenth century technology was being developed to wash and clean coal, allowing maximum coal recovery. At Murton, around 1892, a revolving stream washer was introduced, using around 450 gallons of water a minute, and processing 400 tons of coal per day.[73] Bolckow and Vaughan sent their Dean and Chapter coal to a Graham and Morton screen, erected in 1904–5, before transferring the material to a huge Belgian 'Coppee' washery,[74] while at the Horden Collieries the small coal was processed in a 'Baum' jig washery, before being sent to the coke ovens.[75] This dealt with coal smaller than 1½ in across. Anything between 1½ in and 8 in was sent separately to a dense medium plant for cleaning. The slurry from the Baum washery and the dense medium plant underwent further processing by froth flotation, and was converted into cake for the coke ovens. Thrislington Colliery used another type, the 'Luhrig' jig system, while at Murton, W.O. Wood, the agent of the South Hetton and Murton

Reprocessing at Waterhouses' pit heaps in the 1920s.

Coal Company, and Burnett, the engineer, created their own washery, which was taken up by the mining market .[76] By 1929, 560 washeries had been built in Britain – 154 in Scotland, 108 in South Wales, and 38 in Durham. During that year the Durham plants washed 6,256,000 tons of coal. Horden Colliery also had the facilities, certainly in 1930, to dry-clean 250 tons of coal an hour.[77]

Around the pit yard were various buildings associated with the running of the colliery. The colliery office might be at the pit, though at some mines it was in a converted house in one of the rows of miners' houses. Here the manager worked, and discussed operations with his officials. Clerks were also employed to deal with the paper-work and pay. Other buildings included the various workshops of the mechanics, stables, and the lamp cabin.

The mechanics undertook work on the surface and below ground at the pit, but also maintained colliery-owned buildings, including the miners' houses. This group included masons, fitters, joiners, tubmenders, sawyers, wagonwrights, painters, blacksmiths, boilersmiths, smiths, strikers, farriers, plumbers, saddlers and electricians.

(opposite) Above, Sherburn Hill Colliery pit heap, 1957; below, aerial flight erected at Easington, 1953.

The masons undertook bricklaying, stonework (drystone and mortared walling), and slating and tiling of colliery houses. When necessary they undertook the lining and maintainance of the shaft, and underground construction work. Mr George Stewart, a mason at South Hetton from 1940 to

A Simon-Carvès Baum washery, Horden, 1937.

1980, recalled that at some underground locations where they were working, they had to walk in about 3½ miles carrying their tools, twenty-five minutes a mile being the allowed travelling time. On one occasion, stonemen had cleared an open space, and the masons built an underground hauler engine house 60 ft long, 40 ft wide and 18 ft high, with 2 ft thick walls to take the girders. Scaffolding had to be carried inbye for use during bricklaying. The masons also constructed stoppings used in the control of air flow. The walls were laid, and set into the sides of the rock, before being plastered over to prevent the seepage of gas. The stoppings had to be a minimum of 14 in thick due to the pressure of the roof. During this work the mason would have had a safety lamp with him.

The blacksmiths undertook the necessary metalwork – manufacturing, replacing and renewing items for constructional work, track, and machinery. The miner's pick, both hand and pneumatic, also needed sharpening at frequent intervals, and 'pick-sharpeners' did this, along with any other smith work. In 1899 they were alloted a basic wage of 2s. 6d. a day, with contributions, known as 'pick pence', from the men. In 1938 lower-paid sharpeners had their wage raised to the mechanics' county standard. Tubs, which were either of wood with a metal frame and wheels, or completely metal, also needed occasional repairs.

Maintenance of the shaft was usually undertaken at weekends by 'shaftsmen', who were generally mechanics. Wearing a harness, they travelled in the shaft on the top of the cage, using a pull-wire to signal to the winding engineman – one rap to stop, two to go up, and three to go down. It was possible to transfer men and materials from one cage roof to another, when they were level (at 'the meetings' shown by the winding-engineman's indicator). Their work included repairing or replacing the 8 in x 4 in pitch pine buntings, replacing cage ropes and checking the water pressure behind the tubbing.

Heavy horses were used for haulage purposes, but by the first decade of the twentieth century they had largely been replaced by mechanical means. Putting ponies of 10 to 11 hands, and driving ponies of 12 to 13 hands, continued to be used. Shetland and Welsh breeds were usually purchased, and in some cases reared until they were about five years of age.[78] A farrier then broke the animal, and trained it for its future work. When ready, the animal would be lowered down the shaft in a harness or net. Once down the pit the new pony would sometimes have two drivers, until it gained experience. The majority of ponies accepted their fate, but some were temperamental. One fifteen-year-old boy was kicked in the face by a restive pony at the Dorothy Pit at Lambton in 1927, and needed hospital treatment.[79] There were occasional incidents of ill-treatment of ponies, but culprits were punished if caught, and sometimes taken to court. However, on the whole, pit ponies were treated kindly. At some drift mines the ponies were brought out at holidays, but at deeper pits, like Stargate, the ponies only came to bank when they were dead.[80]

When there were pit disasters, the ponies frequently died along with the

Pony in an underground stable, possibly Brancepeth or Kibblesworth.

Boys with pit ponies wearing leather caps, Brancepeth 'A' Pit, 1929.

men. At the Tudhoe explosion in 1882, sixty-eight of the eighty-three horses and ponies were killed by the force of the explosion, or by the fire and gas. In 1896 Thomas Carling, aged fourteen, and Bartholomew Newell, fifteen, were asphyxiated by afterdamp in the Brancepeth explosion. Their bodies were found by the Jet seam stables, near their dead horses. As the animals' bodies were brought out one boy said:

> 'Ye see that galloway, Sir. . . ,' pointing to a carcass, 'Weel, that was my galloway – the best I iver'drove – the best in the pit!'. . . Then, as chief mourner, he followed his dead favourite to its burial place and remained until the earth covered it from sight.[81]

A farrier was normally in overall charge of the ponies, and of a number of horsekeepers, usually one for every twelve to sixteen ponies. Stabling was provided above and below ground, and hay and fodder had to be taken underground, just as the dung had to be cleared and brought out in tubs. The animals' life and work was carefully supervised, and particular care was taken of blind ponies.

The miners' safety lamp was the property of the colliery owner, and damage to the lamp had to be reported and paid for. Special lamp cabins were erected above ground for the storage and maintenance of the mens' lamps, which were numbered. Until well into the 1880s it was common practice for the miner, after his shift, to leave the burner-reservoir section of the lamp at the cabin, for filling and cleaning, while taking the upper half home.[82] Gradually this custom was done away with, and the whole lamp was left. The

Mr George James, farrier at the Hutton stables, Brancepeth 'A' Pit, 1929.

staff in the cabin cleaned and maintained the lamps, and filled them with oil. This was either whale oil, or a vegetable form, like 'colza' rape oil, or the petroleum derivative 'colzalene'. Although colzalene produced a bright light, it was particularly volatile, and lamp cabins were consequently well ventilated. The flame lamp was lit and locked for the men at the start of their shift, and when battery-powered lamps came into use, the lamp cabin men put them on charge at the end of the miners shift, ready for the next day.

CHAPTER 3

Coke-Making

The bituminous coals of the Durham coalfield had a high carbon content and were particularly suited for conversion to coke. West Durham coke, in particular, achieved a world-wide reputation for quality, and many collieries had associated coke-yards.

At the colliery crushed coal was filled into special tubs holding about 18 cwt, which were then pushed by men called 'small-runners' along gantrys to the batteries of coke ovens. The small-runner moved the tub along overhead rails by running on low plates or planks – an athletic task, as the

Hamsteels beehive coke-yard, 1923. Hamsteels had been worked by Joseph Johnson, but in the 1920s it was taken over by Sir S.A. Sadler, who had interests in both the chemical and coal industries.

Coke-yard workers at Bitchburn.

plates were narrow, and the runner could easily fall onto the oven domes. The runner then positioned the tub over the mouth of the oven, a slide was removed from the base of the tub, and the coal funnelled into the oven. Six or seven tub loads were usually required to charge each oven. The front door was built up by a 'leveller' using fireclay blocks, the payment in 1908 being 3s. 4d. for each door. Young 'dauber lads' supplied the mortar, prepared in a pug mill, which was used to bind the blocks together. During this work the levellers spread the coal using long rakes, ensuring that the fine and rough coals were equally mixed and properly levelled to ensure an even burn. Eventually the door and the charging hole were totally sealed once the gas had flamed.

An experienced 'burner' regulated the flow of air to the oven, ensuring that its mixture with the gases from the coal produced the right state of combustion to form a bright, hard and dense coke. The ovens would be left to burn, with occasional checks at various times of the day and night to ensure that everything was all right.

After forty-eight, or even ninety-six hours, the oven would be ready to draw. Under the supervision of the burner, the 'drawer' would carefully take down the fireclay blocks of the door, saving them for re-use. He then inserted a hose-pipe into the furnace, and sprayed the oven's contents. This process was called 'slaking'. There was a particular technique to the spraying, applying the water in the right direction to ensure proper cooling, while

avoiding over-watering, which would destroy the coke, and under-watering, allowing the coke to retain fire, thus requiring further watering which could turn it into useless ballast.

Once the cooling was complete, the drawer used a heavy shovel or 'peel', fixed to a bar and balance, to remove the coke by forcing the shovel into the oven and hauling out the coke onto a bench which ran the length of the row of ovens. A drawer normally cleared three 11 ft ovens in a working day.

'Fillers' brought empty trucks from the colliery sidings to the bench, the track-bed being much lower than the level of the bench, enabling the filler to load the trucks more easily. Broad forks (or 'gripes') were often used. The fillers often cleared the coke-roads of any material that had been dropped, though this was sometimes done by general labourers, who also 'riddled' (sieved) ballast to extract 'breeze' (fine coke).

Due to the nature of the burning process there were no stated hours, and the men were paid on piece-work, the drawers, small-runners and levellers by the oven, the fillers either by the number of trucks loaded or tonnage price. Masons and their labourers were also employed to maintain and repair the ovens. Coke-making gradually resulted in the ovens being coated with clinker. Eventually the surfaces of some of the bricks would decay, and patching or more extensive re-lining had to take place.

In the employment ladder daubers and small-runners could move on to become fillers, but it was the burner who decided if a person was suitable to be taken on as a drawer. It was also the burner who specified the ovens each drawer was to work on during the day.

Increasingly there were moves towards automation. Small engines were used to move charging-tubs to the ovens, and by 1878 Bell Bros had introduced automatic feeding of their beehive ovens at Browney Colliery,

A coke filler at Hamsteels. Fillers generally used broad, sixteen-pronged forks for loading coke into trucks.

Engine and small-runners tubs, Hamsteels.

installing a belt in front of the ovens enabling the coke to be drawn directly onto it.[1] This enabled the drawers to increase the number of ovens cleared in an eight hour day from two to four, with a reduction in labour costs per oven of 7½d.

Developments were also made to the ovens, with underfloor flues to gain a more thorough burn, and the utilization of waste heat by providing a vent at the back of each oven, linked to a main flue which drew the hot gases over boilers, before being emitted into the atmosphere up a tall chimney. Experiments had also been carried out at the Peases West Bankfoot complex in 1860 to try and recover by-products from the gases given off in the carbonization process, particularly ammonia, but these were unsuccessful.[2] In 1882, however, Henry Simon, the founder of Simon-Carvès Limited, installed twenty-five of his ovens at the site.

In Belgium, France and Germany the by-product oven rapidly replaced the beehive, but the idea of by-product recovery was slow to catch on in Britain until around 1903, when more foreign patent ovens were introduced. In 1907 there were Otto-Hilgenstock ovens at Blaydon Burn, St Helens, Templetown, Eldon, New Brancepeth and Leasingthorne; Simon-Carvès

ovens at Peases West, Malton and Bearpark; Semet Solvey ovens at Thrislington; and Belgian Coppee ovens at Dean and Chapter Colliery, Ferryhill. The Pease company installed ninety Otto-Hilgenstock ovens at Bankfoot in 1908, with a coking capacity of 4,000 tons per week.[4] The coal was sent to the yard by aerial ropeway, where it was delivered to coal compressing boxes, each with a capacity equal to charging sixty ovens. The coal was drawn by mechanical ram, automatically quenched on inclined platforms, and transported by conveyor to screens for grading and loading into trucks. After the 1926 strike many of the old beehives were considered to be inefficient and antiquated, and were demolished.

The patent ovens and associated plant were also designed to recover and manufacture products from the destructive distillation of the coal. These included sulphate of ammonia, tar, benzol, solvent naptha, napthalene, xylon and toluol. The gases produced in the coking process were extracted by exhausters and piped to chemical works. At Malton Colliery, near Lanchester, seventy Simon-Carvès ovens were erected around 1893, and for every ton of coke produced, 7 gallons of tar, 2 gallons of crude benzol and 32 lb of sulphate of ammonia were recovered or produced.[5]

These patent ovens and by-product recovery plants employed a wide range of workers – loaders, levellers, cranemen, doormen, door washers, stampers, ram enginemen, and those employed in valve cleaning, regulating

Patent ovens at Bankfoot, Crook. Henry Simon built by-product ovens here in 1882, and in 1908 120 Otto waste heat by-product ovens were added to the coking operations.

North Brancepeth
Colliery and coke-yard.

A coke-car at North
Brancepeth.

gas burners, dealing with the centrifuge, hydraulic mains, exhausters and scrubbers, and in the processing of sulphate of ammonia, benzol and tar distilling.[6]

After the 1926 strike, many of the beehive coke ovens were shut down, though production at other plants continued at a high level, with about a quarter of the county's coal output being carbonized. In 1944 Durham produced 4,544,419 tons of coke, out of a UK total of 14,061,354 tons, coke production being concentrated at twenty-four sites between the Tyne and Tees.[7]

Following the nationalization of the coal industry, a £2 million coking plant was established at Fishburn in May 1954.[7] Four years later two batteries of Woodall-Duckham Becker Combination Underjet ovens were erected at Hawthorn.[8] It was officially known as the Murton coking plant, and was capable of producing 250,000 tons of coke annually, along with ammoniacal liquor, tar and around a million gallons of crude benzol.

Murton and Fishburn formed part of an NCB subsidiary, National Smokeless Fuels Limited, a producer of foundry, blast furnace and domestic coke, including 'Sunbrite' smokeless fuel. During the early 1960s, a series of cokeworks were closed, such as Langley Park, Stella Gill and Trimdon Grange, and in the early 1980s the county saw an over-production of coke, and a decline in the markets for it, the latter partly due to a slump in steel manufacturing and the importation of foreign coke to centres like the Redcar Steelworks.[9] As a result, Fishburn was closed down in October 1986. Monkton, the last cokeworks, closed in 1990 due to a concerted campaign by local residents who opposed the level of pollution from the plant, and its effects on health.

Lambton cokeworks. This plant had Semet Solway waste heat and Simplex regenerative ovens. These were replaced in the late 1930s by Collin silica regenerative ovens.

CHAPTER 4

Major Disasters and Miners' Safety

Working in tunnels below the ground has obvious inherent dangers, with roof collapses, accidents during the haulage process, inundation, gas, inhalation of dust and explosions.

One of the most frequent causes of accidents and deaths in mines were roof falls. Taking as one example the three-year period 1876-8, there were 116 deaths in the Durham coalfield from stone falls.[1] An inquest on the death of John Maguire, who was killed in the Five Quarter seam of the Bute

A roof collapse which killed Mr J. Nicholson, Brancepeth 'A' Pit.

Pit at Tanfield Lee in 1927, provides just one example. A newspaper report of the evidence given by Martin Pattison, a pony puter, stated that:

> a baulk and some stones had fallen at the top end of the landing. Suspecting that there might be a further fall, he went back to the coal face and told the six hewers, including Maguire, and they returned to the landing together. Witness said he would go and seek the deputy, and just as he spoke the top came down completely, burying Maguire and witness's right foot. He managed to free himself, and informed the deputy overman what had happened.
>
> John Keelor, the deputy overman, said that when he reached the fall the landing was completely closed up. He shouted 'Hello, Johnny?' and received an answer 'Hello! I am done.' Witness shouted back 'Keep your heart up Johnny. We will not be long before we get to you'. Rescue operations were commenced without delay, and witness spoke to Maguire periodically between 5.30 and 11.45 p.m. The last reply he had from Maguire was at 11.45 p.m., when he said very faintly: 'Hello, I am done.' Maguire was dead when the fall was cleared away from him at 3.55 a.m. on Saturday. There were marks of injuries upon the head and face.[2]

Broompark Colliery fire, 1904.

A number of serious fires destroyed surface facilities, particularly at Broompark,[3] Thrislington,[4] South Pelaw and South Moor.[5]

North Brancepeth Coal Company's Broompark Colliery was about to be 'laid-in' when fire broke out at the screens on the 8 August 1904. It was first discovered at 7.45 p.m., and the steam buzzer was signalled. About twelve men and boys who were working in the drift escaped with the ponies, but within a quarter of an hour the heapstead was engulfed. Stacks of pit props and nearby coal wagons caught fire, as did the pumping-engine-house. Langley Moor fire brigade arrived quickly, but at 9 o'clock the screens fell, throwing clouds of sparks and burning debris into the air. At 10 p.m. the pulleys of the headstock collapsed. Luckily, the fan-house, which supplied air to the nearby Littleburn Colliery, was saved.

A serious fire also occurred at Thrislington Colliery in 1911. The North Bitchburn Coal Company had only purchased it about two years before, at a cost of £65,000, and were working the Harvey and Busty with 400 hands. It was thought that a paraffin lamp in the enginehouse exploded, and the fire spread to the heapstead and the uprights of the main and return shafts. The screens then caught alight, and the cages fell down the shaft. Sixty-seven ponies were underground at the time, but when the officials were lowered by 'crab' (winder) down the back shaft they found the ponies alive, and the

The wreckage of Broompark Colliery.

workings unaffected. The damage was estimated at £7,000, but was covered by insurance.

South Pelaw heapstead caught fire in 1911, with eighty-four men and boys underground in the Busty seam. The officials turned the fan off, to prevent smoke entering the workings, and the workers were brought out safely. In the same year a fire broke out in the enginehouse, and spread to the new pit head of the Charley Pit, South Moor, causing serious damage.

Pit shafts have been the scenes of a series of accidents in County Durham. At Kelloe, new four-decker cages had been installed in 1910. During one operation the brakesman had brought the full cage from the Hutton seam some distance up the shaft, when, it is said, the rope socket came away from the cage top, resulting in the cage dashing back down.[6] The descending cage, containing empty tubs, also came loose, the rope flying off the drum in the engine-house. The cages smashed through 16 in x 14 in buntings placed across the shaft and smashed into the sump of the Harvey seam.

Fortunately the cages were empty in this incident. However, at 3.30 one October morning in 1862 two boys, who had been at work all night at Hedleyhope Colliery, entered the cage to return to bank.[7] Accidentally the cage was drawn right up to the pulley wheels, into a slanting position, with the result that both boys fell down the 132 ft shaft.

At Consett Iron Company's South Medomsley Colliery the Busty downcast shaft took two cages. On 24 February 1923 the banksman signalled to the onsetter that it was time to send up the foreshift men who worked at the shaft bottom siding – two onsetters and six lads.[8] They got into the North double-decker cage and had risen part of the way up the shaft when a worn cage shoe came off the guide rail. The cage tipped over in the shaft, and the occupants fell to their deaths.

Inundations of water have also occurred at several collieries, including East Hetton Colliery in 1897,[9] and Sacriston in 1903.[10] At the latter pit, men were working in the third west district of the Busty, where there was a hitch between it and the Fulforth district, which had been standing about eight years. Water had accumulated in the Fulforth and broke through into the third west 2nd north flat with great force. John Whittaker and Thomas McCormick were caught by the inrush and were killed instantly, and the water quickly rose to a depth of about 5 ft. Robert Richardson, who had been working in a slightly higher area than that of the other men, saw the water coming in, and quickly tipped a tub over and stacked timber on it, and then climbed onto it himself, out of reach of the surrounding water. Eventually his lamp went out, but he kept tapping on the side of the tub. Rescue workers, wading up to their necks in water, found the bodies of Whittaker and McCormick, and heard Richardson tapping. He was eventually located and brought out of the mine, having been trapped for eighty-eight hours.

In coalmining the most dangerous gases are methane (firedamp) and carbon monoxide. Methane is associated with the fossilized vegetation which is

Sacriston Colliery in the 1920s. Sacriston, and the associated Charlaw Colliery, were operating from the 1840s and produced coal suitable for conversion to foundry and blast furnace coke.

the basis of coal, and may be emitted when a new face is exposed. Because it is a light gas, it tends to occur in the roof area, and may linger in the goaf. When there is a drop in atmospheric pressure, the gas tends to expand. Consequently, a deputy was required to check the barometer at the pit head as he started his inspection. If present, the gas could be detected with a flame safety lamp, its presence being indicated by a pale 'cap' over the flame, the greater the quantity of gas, the higher the cap. The Coal Mines General Regulations (Firedamp Detectors), 1939, specified where detectors were to be placed during a shift. By the 1950s the 'Spiralarm' was in use at Easington.[11] If firedamp was present in the atmosphere, the fixed flame within the device would increase in intensity, heating a metal spiral which would expand and trigger off a flashing light.

A common feature associated with explosions is the presence of carbon monoxide, produced by the burning of carbon and limited supplies of oxygen. This 'afterdamp' was colourless, odourless and tasteless, and could not be detected by a safety lamp. If breathed in, it affected the circulation of oxygen through the bloodstream. The victim would suffer headache, sickness, and would, within a short space of time, collapse and die, if not rescued in time. The only way that the gas could be detected was by taking a caged canary into the area, and noting if the bird was affected.

Where there was an explosion of firedamp, it was found that the destructive power could be dramatically increased if it came into contact with coal dust. It was found that ignition would occur if a pound of coal dust was mixed with 160 cubic ft of air. This propensity was identified by Professors

A scene from the flooding at Sacriston Colliery, 1903.

Faraday and Lyall in their investigation of the explosion in the Meadows Flat of the Little Pit at Haswell in 1844, when ninety-five were killed. Once the dangers of coal dust had been accepted, and it took a long time, considerable efforts were made to try and suppress it. The general practice was to water dusty areas. This was sometimes done by running a tub of water along the road, with holes in the base which allowed the water to sprinkle out. In other cases it was done by men with buckets of water and scoops. At some collieries, such as Murton, the material forming the roof and sides made watering an unsafe option, because of the danger of the material bulging and falling in. At Bolckow, Vaughan and Company's collieries men were specifically employed to go around, removing coal dust from the roof, timbers and sides onto the road with handbrushes.[12] The road could then be watered, and the accumulated sludge removed. Later it was found that stone dust, spread in the working area and in areas where shots were to be fired, markedly reduced the possibilities of coal dust ignition. At Lambton Colliery stone band was burnt in the pit boilers, using a patent forced draught system, and the waste stone dust was used for the roadways.[13]

Surface operations, like the tipplers discharging coal down to the screens, also produced dust, and overhead extractors were used to cope with this. With the increasing use of conveyors, the level of dust produced was minimized by installing water sprinklers by the belt. Experiments were also undertaken at Easington in the 1950s with foam to blanket any underground fires.

Dust got into wounds and left a blue-black stain in the scar, and this same dust produced the most insidious of the occupational effects, the fibrosis of the lungs, pneumoconiosis, due to its inhalation. Engels, in 1844, wrote of the saturation of the miners' lungs with dust, the black mucous expectoration and coughing.[14] Dust was produced in hand picking and blasting, but the introduction of machinery into the pits increased the dust. A hewer working in a low seam cutting coal with a 'windy pick' found that the coal dust in such a confined space just blew back into his face. Inhalation resulted in

Experiments in fire suppression, Easington, 1954.

Fire control using foam, Easington, 1954.

gradual debility, and, to take just one example, a miner died of heart failure as a result of pneumoconiosis, thirteen years after his dust-filled lungs had become a problem. A study of miners at ten pits around the coalfield in 1967 revealed that of the 13,290 men examined (27.6 per cent of the county's mineworkers), 1,303 were, in some way, disabled. Of this group, the main form of disability was pneumoconiosis, found in 385 men (29.6 per cent).[15]

Sadly, the pits of County Durham have experienced a considerable number of explosions, and the following examples record some of the major disasters. They recall not only the great dangers under which the miner worked, and the horror of underground explosions and gas, but also the bravery of the miners, officials and rescue teams who risked, and in several cases gave, their own lives to save their fellow pitmen.

Seaham Colliery, 1880

The Marquis of Londonderry's Seaham Colliery comprised two pits, the Seaham or Low Pit, and the Seaton High Pit or 'Nicky Nack'.[16] About 1,400 hands were employed in raising 2,500 tons of gas coal a day, mainly from the Hutton seam, though the Main, Maudlin and Harvey were also worked.

On Wednesday 8 September 1880, at about 2 a.m., the firing of a shot in an area of coal dust caused an explosion in the Maudlin. The noise was heard at the High and Low pit heads, and the ground shook, waking people in the village. This brought crowds to the scene, and miners and officials quickly formed into search parties. The shaft and cage had been damaged,

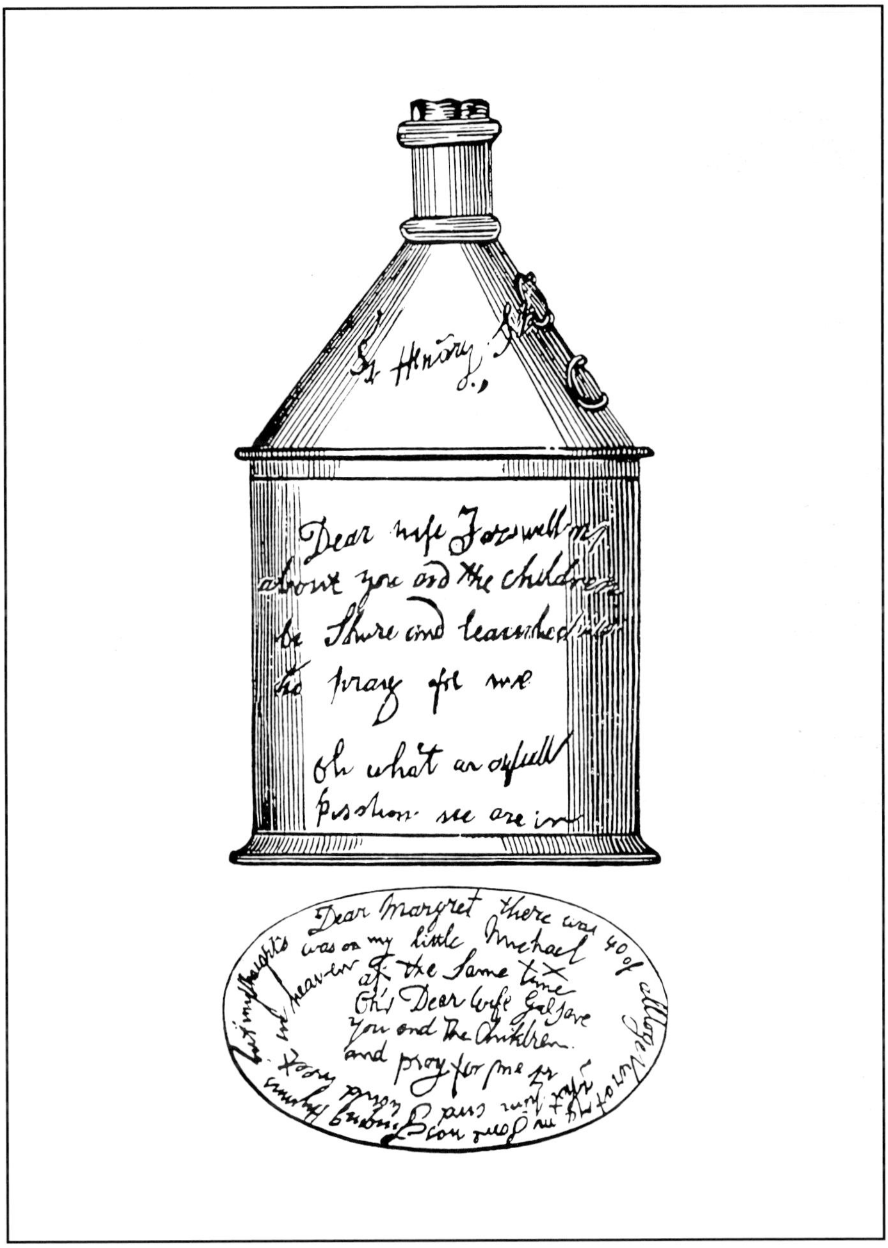

Michael Smith's inscribed water bottle, Seaham disaster, 1880.

and there were tons of debris blown about. This material had to be cleared first, before the rescuers could descend on ropes.

At the Maudlin seam the engine-house and stables were found to be on fire, and these had to be put out before exploration could begin. All the ponies had suffocated; further through the seam lay debris and mutilated bodies. The area of the 'Drop Staple' was 'almost torn to pieces', and the rescuers held camphor bags between their teeth as they located body after body.

A week later the team located George Dixon, a shifter, who had been entombed. They called to him to climb over the fall, but he told them that a driver-boy lay injured with him and couldn't move, and he wouldn't leave him. Two days after that the rescuers broke through and found the child clasped in the shifter's arms. Both were dead.

In the Hutton seam all the miners had died from the afterdamp. The searchers then had the appalling task of recovering the bodies. With the effect of the gas, and having lain for several days, the bodies had swollen and partly decomposed. The searchers were forced to wear respirators and shoulder-length leather gloves as they placed the remains into canvas body-bags, and covered them with disinfectant. They were then transferred to the kibble and brought to bank. In all, 168 men and boys died.

When the body of Michael Smith was brought back to his wife, she found his water-bottle clasped under his arm. On it, at different times, he had scratched messages:

> Dear Margaret, There was forty of us altogether at 7am. Some was singing hymns, but my thoughts were on my little Michael. I thought that him and I would meet in heaven at the same time. Oh dear wife, God save you and the children, and pray for myself; Dear Wife, farewell, my last thought bout you and the children. Be sure and learn them to pray for me; Oh what an awfull position we are in.[17]

Michael Smith's son, who was ill when his father left for work, died the same day as the explosion.

Trimdon Grange Colliery, 1882

Trimdon Grange Colliery was sunk in 1840 and was held, with Kelloe, by the East Hetton Colliery Company, but was then bought by Walter Scott of Newcastle.[18] Trimdon Grange had two shafts, to the Low Main and Harvey, united by a staple, and further linked to Kelloe by a passageway. The colliery was known to be dusty.

On 16 February 1882 barometric pressure was noticeably low, with a recorded temperature drop of 5°F at the pit mouth. The back shift of five deputies, sixty-four hewers and twenty-five boys went down to their work places. A caution board had been put up, so that, outbye, the drivers could use open midgies; inbye, Davy lamps with a sliding shield were used. The state of the roof in the Pit Board Narrow district of the Harvey seam was not good, and some propping had taken place. It is possible that a fall of roof stone in this area forced out gas under pressure into the work places, mixing with coal dust, and igniting over a Davy lamp, though the later inquiry failed to reach a definite conclusion. Some warning of danger existed, for three men made an attempt to escape from their places before they died, as the pit exploded at 2.40 p.m. The seat of the disaster seems to have been at the southern end of the Second South, and all the workers in the Pit Board Narrow district were killed. Most of them died either through the violence of

Trimdon Grange lodge banner. The design is of representatives of England, Scotland, Wales and Ireland clasping hands in a gesture of unity. On the reverse side of the banner is a depiction of the 'bundle of sticks' fable, and the motto 'Unity is strength'.

the explosion or by being burnt, although workers away were also severely burnt. 'The afterdamp left victims scattered from end to end of the mine'.

The explosion damaged the cage and ropes, and the dividing door in the Trimdon–Kelloe passage was blown out. A search party began clearing the debris in the Harvey shaft, cleared the cage, and worked their way in to the seams. The thirty hewers in the Low Main were unhurt and were brought to bank.

Herman Schier, the undermanager at Kelloe, led a team from the Kelloe Colliery end, in the hope of reaching any survivors. They worked their way through the connecting passage but as they progressed they were caught by the afterdamp. Thomas Blenkinsopp, the master-wasteman, collapsed, and Schier, attempting to pull him out, also fell. The others in the team eventually dragged them out, but both were dead.

With Schier, and those killed at Kelloe, seventy-four men and boys died as a result of the explosion. Amongst them were three brothers – George Burnett, a nineteen-year-old shaftsman, whose clothes and head had been blown off; James, a seventeen-year-old landing minder, who was only identifiable by his clothing; and Joseph, a twenty-three-year-old hand putter, whose body was found later in the search.[19] The brothers were specifically mentioned in Tommy Armstrong's well-known poem on the 'Trimdon Grange Explosion', which appealed for aid for the widows and orphans:

> Let us think of Mrs. Burnett,
> Once had sons but now has none,
> By the Trimdon Grange explosion
> Joseph, George and James are gone.

Tudhoe Colliery, 1882

Tudhoe Colliery was owned by the Weardale Iron & Coal Company. This firm had blast furnaces at Tow Law, with forges and mills at Tudhoe. Along with Tudhoe, they worked coal at West Thornley, Black Prince, Hedley Hill, Croxdale, and the Charles and Eden pits at Middridge.

Under the management of William Johnson, the Brockwell, Busty and Hutton seams were worked at Tudhoe by bord and pillar, to produce coking coal and some gas coal.[20] The pit was considered fiery, and a caution board demarcated the areas safe for naked lights, and those where Davy, Geordie and Clanny lamps were needed. This caution board was normally illuminated by a lamp set up by the deputy, and put out by him when work finished. The lamp was to play a part in the discussion at the later inquiry.

It was suggested that gas appeared, from some source, perhaps from a fall of stone, and entered the Brockwell workings. Around 1.15 a.m. on 18 April 1882 men firing a shot in stone to enlarge a doorway may have ignited it. There was, however, doubt as to this being the cause, as there should have been a good current of air in that place. Alternatively, the gas came from the goaf, and, it was suggested, ignited over the lamp at the caution board, though certain depositions made at the inquiry indicated that the deputy had already put the lamp out.

From whatever source, the blast hit a man-riding set of forty-four tubs carrying six men. All were burnt to death and, as the timbering collapsed, a heavy roof-fall covered several of the bodies. In all, thirty-five died in the Brockwell as a result of the explosion, of whom twenty-two died from burns, several charred beyond recognition, twelve from the afterdamp, and one from violent force and afterdamp.

The blast was heard a mile away, and rescue teams quickly arrived. John Nesbit, the fore-overman, and William White, the night-shift overman, went into the No. 6 West Pit, where they knew boys had been working, but, sadly, both men were caught by the afterdamp and killed.[21]

Elemore Colliery, 1886

Elemore Colliery, worked by the Hetton Coal Company, was not considered gassy.[22] At the George Low Main seam a brick-arched main intake led off from the shaft, with a branch road, the Dale Way, 520 ft along it. It was proposed to extend the arched way, and a team was sent down at 4 p.m. on 1 December 1886 to shoot out stone to undertake this work. No gas was found, and there were no problems with the firing. Three men took over at 11 p.m. One shot was fired in a machine-drilled hole, and later, at around 2.55 a.m. on the 2nd, a further shot was fired in a hand-drilled hole near the floor. This shot appears to have caused the explosion of gas from an unidentified source.

The blast went outbye to the shaft, blowing flame up it, and showering dust over the December snow. It also went down the shaft into the workings of the Lyons Low Main, killing the furnace-man, and then down to the Lady Low Main, burning two men to death, though six others escaped. In the lower Lady Hutton, it shot 1,122 yards through to the face. Seven men there were burnt, suffocated by coal dust, or killed by shock or afterdamp. The blast also went inbye through most of the workings, killing some men by force and fire, while others fell to the afterdamp. Twenty-eight died.

(opposite) Above, crowds at Wingate Grange, 1906; below, families at Wingate Grange waiting for news.

Wingate Grange Colliery, 1906

Wingate Grange Colliery employed 1,338 hands, 1,116 of them underground, working the Five Quarter, Low Main, Hutton and Harvey.[23] There were two shafts, the Lord and Lady. On Sunday 14 October 1906 the stonemen and shifters had gone down during the evening, and a man called Maddison had been sent by the master-shifter to clear a small roof fall. Maddison was an experienced pitman and a licensed shot-firer. For some inexplicable reason he decided to remove a projecting area of stone on the side of the main haulage road, a piece of stone which had been like that for twenty-five years without being a hindrance. Without moving the prop

below it, he placed a charge of geloxite (basically nitro-glycerine) on top of the stone, and stemmed it with greasy coal dust. On firing the charge, the spark ignited coal dust. At 11.40 p.m. a low rumbling sound was heard in the village and for several miles around. The blast had extended up the staple to the Five Quarter, while also damaging the Hutton and Harvey seams, entombing the men there. Those in the Low Main were killed by the explosion, while those in the Five Quarter were caught by the afterdamp. Ben Johnson, a shifter in the Low Main, felt the blast and, realizing that afterdamp was coming through, shouted 'Run for your lives, lads!'.[24] Terror-stricken, they ran, tripping over a body and the carcass of a pony that had been blown from its limbers, only to find one route blocked by a collapse. The gas was rising; Harry Pace fell, and though dragged by his friends, died in their arms. Then they fled, and reached the upcast shaft as the rescue team arrived.

Twenty-four men died, their average age being fifty-one years. Their bodies were brought to the joiners shop and laid in two long rows on the work benches for identification. A sandstone memorial now stands in the village to commemorate the dead.

Glebe Pit, 1908

Washington Coal Company owned the 'F' Pit, and in 1904 sank the Glebe Pit, by means of the freezing process. The upcast and downcast shafts were sunk to the Low Main, and there was a stone drift up to the Maudlin seam. Ventilation was supplied by a 25 ft Waddle fan at bank, by the upcast shaft.

On 20 February 1908 the fore and backshift hewers had been at work, overlapped by the haulage workers, and at night the stonemen and repairers came in.[25] The bottom stone was normally shot up to make tub height, and the top canch on the main haulage roads was shot down during the night shift. A permitted explosive, Bellite No. 1, with a No. 7 detonator, was used with multi-firing capability. A hole was properly drilled into the pavement,

Wingate Grange Lodge banner, draped in black, during the funeral service.

(opposite) The victims of the Glebe disaster, 1908

DURHAM MINE DISASTER.
AT THE GLEBE COLLIERY WASHINGTON
AMBROSE MADDON
THOMAS APPLEGARTH.
EDWARD ASHMAN.
ROBERT COWAN.
HARRY OSWALD.
WILLIAM HENRY ROLLIN.
CHARLES CHIVERS.
ALFRED WOOD.
JOHN DIXON.
THOMAS McNALLY.
WILLIAM GLENDINNING.
JAMES WAKE.
THOMAS ERRINGTON.
JOHN CLARK.
WHERE 14 MEN WERE KILLED.
THURSDAY FEBRUARY 20TH 1908.
BLISHED BY WHOLESALE TRADING CO., 47, BIGG MARKET, NEWCASTLE-ON-TYNE.

Washington Glebe Pit.

and the charge inserted, stemmed with clay. There had not been any watering of the area, and the surroundings were dusty. The shot-firer, using an electric battery, fired the Bellite No. 1, causing a flame which ignited firedamp and the coal dust. Nine men in the Low Main were killed by the shock of the explosion, five others died from carbon monoxide poisoning.

West Stanley Colliery, 1909

At the Burn Pit at West Stanley in 1909 it seems that, during a roof fall in the goaf, firedamp was expelled and transmitted by air current. Although locked safety lamps were in use, other, unsafe, lamps were also used, and the firedamp seems to have ignited over these lamps.[26] A newspaper correspondent recorded the event:

> A loud report was heard, followed by one much louder, and by a mass of yellow flame which rose to the top of the shaft and to a height, it is estimated, of fifteen feet above the pulleys. It spread some distance around, scorching some of the men who were working at bank. The tale of terror was rapidly spread abroad, and thousands of men, women and children gathered around the pit heap, crowding right across the railway . . . there was no lack of volunteers for searching, officials from many local collieries, as well as the officials and men belonging to the colliery, being quickly on the scene, all eager to render what help was in their power to give. The necessary work of repairing the shaft made the rescue mission extremely prolonged. The shafting was terribly wrecked, and relays of brave men kept hard at work for several hours trying to reach the seams where the men had been employed. Through the long night hundreds of anxious people stood their ground outside the pit awaiting news.

West Stanley Colliery, 1909.

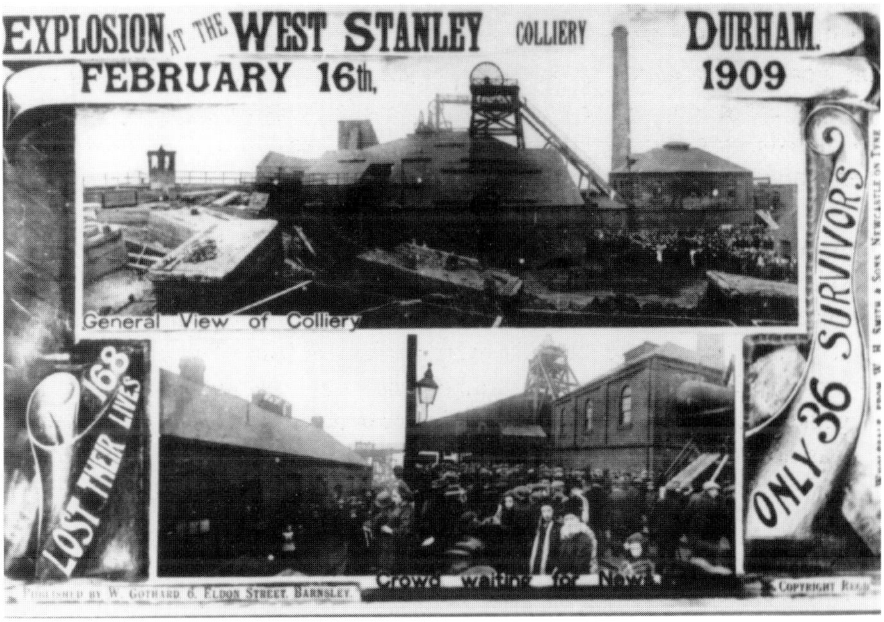

Commemorative card of the West Stanley disaster, 1909.

The mass grave, West Stanley.

William Gardner and pony, rescued from the West Stanley Pit.

(opposite) Crowds at West Stanley waiting for news.

The suspense which held vast crowds around the pit on Tuesday night and all day Wednesday gave way by Wednesday night to a recognition of the worst, and the words 'No hope' were to be read on the countenances of the brave men engaged in fighting to save even one more precious life, though all was done that mortal man could do in the effort to rescue the entombed men.

On the Thursday the worst was known, and the grim work of bringing up the dead bodies of the victims – happily in a small way relieved by the extraction of half a dozen living ponies from the mine – was carried on without interruption.[27]

The explosion had blown through the Busty, Brockwell and Townley seams, killing 168 men and boys. Fifty-nine of the dead were under twenty years of age.

Murton Colliery, 1942

Murton Colliery was owned by the South Hetton Coal Company. In 1942 the Five-Quarter seam, 4 ft 9 in of hard steam coal, was being worked.[28] It was reached by a stone drift, through a drop fault, from the Main coal seam. On Friday 26 June 1942 there were thirteen men in the Back-over Flat during the third shift – two stonemen and a stone putter in the stone drift, two stonemen and a putter at the bottom canch of the middle drift, two fillers and the deputy in the Back drift, two cuttermen in No. 1 Wall, and two fillers in No. 2 Wall. A shot was fired at 8 p.m. in an area where firedamp and air had mixed. The firedamp exploded at the face and became mixed with coal dust, though it was confined to a limited area. A putter in the inbye end of the landing survived, along with a shaken landing lad, but the thirteen men near the face were killed. Carbon monoxide was the main cause of death.

Louisa Pit, 1947

The Louisa Pit worked the middle series seams, with the upper seams worked from the Hedley Colliery, and the lower seams from Morrison Busty.[29] Firedamp appeared from strata below the Hutton seam and mixed with air causing an inflammable mixture. During the night-shift on 22 August 1947 someone brought contraband material into the mine and struck a match to light a cigarette. This initially resulted in a small explosion which, however, progressed and increased in violence as it mixed with coal dust. Twenty-four men were working in the Hutton; nineteen were killed and two others died later in Newcastle Infirmary.

Easington Colliery, 1951

On 29 May 1951 the pick blade of a coal-cutter at a retreating longwall face struck pyrites, causing a spark which ignited firedamp, forced out under roof

Bringing out a victim of the Louisa explosion, 1947.

sinkage in the goaf.[30] The explosion was extended by ignition of coal dust from belt conveyors in the so-called 'Duckbill district' of Easington Colliery, about $1^1/_4$ miles from the shaft bottom, 900 ft below ground.

At the shaft bottom, the shaft wagonwayman heard a loud bang, and quickly got the men in the immediate area out, warned the undermanager, and telephoned through to the Duckbill district. There was no reply. The manager was informed, and a call put through to the Houghton-le-Spring rescue station:

> Rescue brigades and ambulance teams were rushed to the colliery after the explosion occurred and throughout the day laboured unceasingly to try and reach the trapped miners, whose road to safety had been blocked by a huge fall of roof over a large area . . .
>
> An eighteen-year-old datal lad, whose lamp had been left behind in the pit,was at first thought to be missing. He was Ronnie Ritchie . . . 'I was working at the shaft bottom,' he said, 'when I heard the explosion- my ears nearly burst with the roar. The lights went out and dust filled the air and I knew something terrible had happened. I was told by the wagonwayman to go straight to the shaft and the onsetter borrowed my lamp to warn men in another part of the district'.
>
> When crowds of people - many of them from surrounding pit villages - showed no sign of leaving the vicinity of the colliery after ten o'clock

The Hutton seam North Return, Easington.

> at night, Mr S. Watson, standing on the top entrance step of a nearby colliery house, quietly advised them to return home and remain in prayer for the rescuers until, 'in God's good time we reach the entombed men with the hope that some may be rescued alive'.
>
> But Mr Watson's 'Good night and God bless' to the crowd did not dismiss them all. Some went away, but many, including relatives who still had not given up hope, remained.[31]

The rescue workers found the atmosphere in the Duckbill full of gas, and had to ventilate, in stages, with fresh air. Two of the team had emphysema and, while working in the gas with their Aerophor respirators, struggled to breathe and inhaled the gas. Both men collapsed and died.

Over several days the bodies of seventy-two miners (four unidentifiable) were brought out and laid in a communal grave in Easington cemetery. The bodies of nine other miners and two rescue workers were buried elsewhere. John Doyle, a hewer from Horden, wrote these lines on the explosion:

> . . . For here beneath dear Durham skies
> live men I understood
> Bound fast in friendship by the ties
> of pitman brotherhood,
> And as I scan the sacred square
> I bless the minds that thought
> To raise to them this garden fair.
> And bless the hand that wrought –

The Easington disaster memorial.

A miner standing, lamp-in-hand
This sight to stir the soul,
And pray that men may understand
That vivid cross in coal.[32]

The official reports on explosions, and the collection and publication of annual statistics on accidents resulted in measures being gradually taken to improve safety, rescue and the medical care of those injured in the mines. These measures were both statutory and self-help.

In 1903 the Durham Mines Inspection District Ambulance League was established, largely through the efforts of Donald Bain, HM Inspector of Mines, who gave a shield for yearly competitions. John Graham, the Coroner for the Chester Ward, also recalled the situation of first aid treatment for mine accidents in the past:

> They were rough and ready methods in the alleviation of suffering. They could only tie up an artery in a rough kind of way. They could not set a fracture; they could not attend to a dislocation nor to any head injuries. The readiest means were used for conveyance and the homes were often not the best. Perhaps a man was put into a farmer's long cart where there was plenty of straw and a few old coats to keep out the rain and cold. Then the nearest doctor was called and he did his best.

Presentation of the Ambulance Shield, Ryhope.

In 1926 Graham offered a competition shield to further the teaching and practice of first aid in the Durham collieries:

> I have not very much longer to live, but I should like before I go hence to know that there has been a great increase in the number of men who have made themselves proficient in this most essential work.[33]

In 1910 the Mines Accidents (Rescue and Aid) Act was introduced, and in the same year the Durham and Northumberland Collieries Fire and Rescue Station was built at Elswick.[34] Other stations were built at Houghton-le-Spring and Crook. Rescue brigades of not less than five people were to be established at a mine. They were to be tough, fit holders of St John Ambulance certificates and have a detailed knowledge of the underground workings. They were also trained in the use of breathing apparatus and in gas testing. Breathing apparatus, canaries, safety and hand lamps, and up-to-date mine plans were to be immediately available to them if an accident occurred.

Breathing apparatus was slow to catch on in Britain. In Durham the earliest instance of such equipment being used practically was at Seaham, following the explosion in 1881, when Fleuss equipment was worn.[35] The 1906 disaster at Courrières in France, and the use of breathing apparatus there, resulted in the testing of various systems in Britain. At Sacriston smoke helmets with pipes linked to bellows were in use by 1910,[36] while at Felling

Safety-men with smoke helmets linked to bellows, Trimdon or Deaf Hill, c. 1910.

Houghton-le-Spring rescue station team with breathing apparatus, lamps, caged canary and 'Novita' oxygen resuscitation kit, 1935.

Colliery the Draegar life-saving apparatus was introduced.[37] The liquid-air Aerophor was also made available at several collieries.

At the Easington disaster of 1951 11 rescue officers, 48 permanent corps men and 291 trained colliery rescue workers were involved. Murton trained 160 ambulancemen, and had their names posted up underground, so that if there was an accident, they could be summoned instantly. They could undertake first aid, and have the person transferred by stretcher to bank, where a doctor would have been called. An ambulance would always be available on-site. Part III of the Coal Mines General Regulations (First Aid), 1930, required a mine owner to keep an ambulance service in constant readiness. As the number of mines decreased, a base was established at Seaham Harbour to cover Vane Tempest, Seaham, Murton and Easington. This service was closed down in 1991, as British Coal turned to the NHS for ambulance cover.

In 1930 the Durham miners purchased Conishead Priory, overlooking Morecambe Bay, as a convalescent home. The centre offered hydrotherapy, and provided a fortnight's recuperation period for sick miners. There was special cheap rail travel for the miner who was chosen by ballot at his colliery, and pocket money was allocated.[38] Peter Lee said at its opening, 'We have passed through the valley of humiliation, and are coming now to the glorious land of hope and comfort'.[39]

EAST AND WEST FRONT, CONISHEAD PRIORY, CONVALESCENT HOME,
FOR DURHAM MINE WORKERS, ULVERSTON
COPYRIGHT

Sent from the convalescent home to Mr Jim Turnbull on 17 January 1937, this poscard bears the message, 'Things A1 here, Joe'.

In 1943 the Miners Welfare Commission acquired the Hermitage, at Chester-le-Street, and in the following year it opened as a rehabilitation centre for miners suffering from fractures, dislocation and similar injuries.[40] There was a gym for special exercises, and electrical treatment was available. The centre took seventy patients free of charge, but in 1951 it was taken over by the Ministry of Health. Two years later medical treatment centres began to be established at collieries.

CHAPTER 5

'Unity is Strength'

Prior to 1869 the miner was employed on a 'Yearly Bond', usually entered into on 5 April when the colliery official read out the rate of pay and the conditions available at the pit.[1] Those who signed up were usually given 2s. 6d. to start work, and the normal system was to pay wages fortnightly, the non-pay week being known as baff-week. Compared with other industries the Durham miner, and particularly the hewers, were on the whole well paid, and the provision of free houses and coal to certain grades of worker was an added incentive for them to work in what were sometimes fairly isolated areas of the county.

But set against this was the considerable fluctuation in the trade which affected employment and the rate of pay, and which resulted in determined efforts by the miners to retain their high wage status.

There was, however, no standard rate of pay even in one pit or in one grade of work. Both piece-work and day wage rates were paid. The quality of the cavil, the geological conditions, the amount of water, the value of the renk and its additional rates, and the efforts made by the worker influenced the amount which appeared at the top of the pay note, before the deductions for pick-sharpening, powder etc. The piece-work wage of the hewer was based on the score of tubs filled, and there was an unerring regularity in the alterations to score price, which often differed from seam to seam. He could also be fined for the amount of stone mixed with the coal. At Brancepeth the full tubs which failed to come outbye with the coal level with the tub top were rejected, and the hewer lost money. At the same pit the coal owner and Methodist preacher, Joseph Love, worked children sixteen hours a day in 1871. If anyone broke the bond he was liable to arrest, trial and imprisonment. If he struck in an attempt to improve conditions, the law was largely against him. If he stood on a picket line, and even looked at a blackleg, it could be construed as coercion under the 1871 Criminal Law Amendment (Violence) Act for which he could receive three months imprisonment.

Several attempts had been made to form a miners union in the north of

Tommy Hepburn and Lawrence Daley, Easington Lodge banner.

England, in the 1830s by Thomas Hepburn, and in the 1840s. The owners succeeded in smashing them, yet the general desire for unity was not quenched. According to John Wilson, four incidents in the 1860s led to the creation of a new union in 1869 – the Mines Regulation and Inspection Act of 1860; the 1862 disaster at Carr and Company's colliery at Hartley in Northumberland; the Brancepeth 'Rocking strike' over filling tubs, in 1863; and most notably the breaking of the Yearly Bond in the courts by

The cancelling of the Yearly Bond, 1869, Monkwearmouth Lodge banner.

W.P. Roberts in 1869.[2] In that same year the Durham Miners' Mutual Association was formed in the Market Hotel in Durham, (henceforth referred to as the DMA), which was to stand the test of time, strike and economic depression.

The DMA was formed as a benefit society, with the aim of improving the running of collieries and the protection of members from injustice. Some, though not all, of the coal owners joined the Durham Coal Owners' Association (DCOA), whose rules were passed in 1879. Their aim was to regulate wages, and to protect themselves against losses due to strikes etc. The DMA's first headquarters was a Gothic building with a high clock tower, built in 1876 in North Road, Durham City, when the union's membership stood at 40,000.[3] In 1913 the membership had risen to 225,000, and with the pressure of increased business, the old hall was vacated, and the union moved into an elaborate Edwardian Baroque structure at Redhills in 1915.[4]

NATIONAL UNION OF MINEWORKERS
DURHAM AREA
MONKWEARMOUTH LODGE
THE LAST GOOD MORNING
WE CLAIM COMPENSATION
IN GOD IS ALL OUR TRUST
MONKWEARMOUTH LODGE

'We succour the widows and orphans', Brancepeth Lodge banner.

Lodges of the DMA were established at individual collieries, and formally comprised a chairman (or president), secretary, treasurer and committee. Each lodge also had a delegate who attended meetings at Redhills and, with several hundred lodges forming the union, the DMA had a massive council chamber, known as 'The Chapel', because of its similarity to the interior of a Methodist chapel.

The first mass meeting of the lodges took place at Wharton Park in Durham in 1871, when around 5,000 people listened to speakers from Scotland, South Yorkshire and Staffordshire.[5] The following year, and for almost every year since, the annual demonstration, or 'Miners' Gala', was held on Durham racecourse. A newspaper correspondent reported the event in June 1872:

> Although several groups of miners from the outlying districts were early on the march, and invaded the quiet city before many of the residents were well out of their beds, there was no material acquisition from the distant collieries for some hours later. The first detachment on foot put in an appearance at the top of North Road about half past seven o'clock; but soon after these had passed into the city, special trains began to arrive in quick succession, bringing heavy contingents from the mines around South Shields, Consett and other equally noted districts of the county. From this time almost continuous streams of miners, wearing part coloured rosettes, made their way down North Road, both sides of which were lined with a dense crowd of spectators, which appeared to take the greatest interest in the progress of the apparent endless procession, which was dotted here and there with bands playing inspiriting music. At intervals in the procession strong men staggered under the weight of new and handsome banners, on by far the majority of which were emblazoned well painted scenes and figures, and in not a few instances adorned with elegant trimmings and tassels.[6]

The Miners' Hall, Redhills, Durham City. The initial designs were produced by H.T. Gradon, of Durham, and completed by E. Rutherford. C. Groves of Chester-le-Street was the contractor.

(opposite) Seeking compensation for mine deaths, Monkwearmouth Lodge banner.

Interior of the council chamber, Redhills. The hall could accommodate nearly 400 delegates.

Crowds and banners on the Racecourse, Miners' Gala, 1920s.

Ryhope band and banner preparing to leave for the Gala, 1908.

Every lodge of the DMA acquired its own banner.[7] These masterpieces of painted art-work and silk were attached to a bar, hooked to end poles which were carried by chosen men. The newspaper correspondent of 1872, observing the painted scenes on the banners, noted that the:

> spirit of the various mottoes, sentiments, couplets etc., were creditable alike to the heads and hearts of the colliers, evincing, as they did, a fair, conciliatory, and even kindly feeling towards their employers'.

These banners had been produced in London, Manchester and Newcastle, but the firm of George Tuthill of London became the most popular supplier of banners to the lodges. While standard pattern-book formulas were sometimes chosen, other designs were particularly distinctive. Lodges changed their banners as old ones became torn, or the representations painted on them became inappropriate. As lodges closed in later years, a banner might be transferred to another lodge which needed one, with only the name altered; or it would be laid up in the Miners Hall in Durham. When there had been a fatal accident at a colliery, the lodge banner would be draped in black when it was paraded at the Gala.

In 1897 the first miners' service was held in Durham Cathedral, through the efforts of Bishop Westcott (the 'Pitman's Bishop'), and it has continued to be an important and moving feature of the 'Big Meeting'.[8] A small group of chosen lodges enter the packed cathedral with their bands and banners at the beginning of the service, and they lead the congregation out at the end.

Hamsteels Lodge banner at the Miners' Gala, c. 1947.

The playing of the miners' hymn, 'Gresford', recalls the dangers of mining, and asks Christ to:

> Look with compassion, and with love
> On all who toil beneath the earth.

The formation of the lodges of the DMA progressed through the efforts of men like William Patterson, the union agent, and Tommy Ramsay, a 'sacrificed man' well known for carrying a crake to attract people to listen to speeches. Their activities occurred during a period of relatively good trade in the British coal industry, but by 1874 a high peak in coal sales was reached, and the need to be competitive and profitable led to a series of demands by the coal owners for reductions in the men's wages. On arbitration these demands were successful, but led to the adoption of a sliding scale throughout the county in 1877.[9] A depressed coal trade in 1878 led to the owners' demands for reductions of 20 per cent and 12 per cent on underground and surface workers' wages. The miners attempted to compromise, but then proposed open arbitration, to which the owners issued notices to quit, and a county coal strike began in 1879.[10]

There were a few initial disturbances as the owners employed blacklegs. At Hamsteels two men went to work, and at the time they were due to come to bank a crowd of around 1,000 people had converged on the colliery. As the police began to move the men from the pit, people in the crowd began throwing stones. The police drew batons and fought their way up to the colliery houses. By that time they were all wounded, and men began to collect pick-axe handles and pokers to take them on, but the arrival of reinforcements quelled the disturbance.[11] At Hamsterley Colliery the blacklegs were visited by strikers who warned them that if they did not cease work, 'Rebecca' would visit them. In fear they left work.

Beamish Air Lodge banner emerging from the cathedral after a Gala service, 1950s. Durham Cathedral appeared on several miners' banners, including that of Vane Tempest, with the motto 'Build your Association firmly and strong'.

These events were, however, limited, and while a number of mass meetings were held throughout the coalfield, no police were needed at them. At a meeting of miners' wives and daughters at Pelton Fell Mrs Walker of Hebburn Colliery said of the miners:

> They asked for nothing but what was right, and if only they put their shoulder to the wheel they would succeed. Let them stick to one thing above all – open arbitration. Let them keep the peace; and if anyone said the men ought to go to work, let them say 'No; we would rather beg as gan back ti the pit'[12]

In an eloquent speech, Mrs Sharp of Pelton said:

> They talk about England being a free country. They say it is a free country, and that our men are free, but I say not; I say it is a land of slavery. We are in slavery. We are driven like the plough and horses in the fields of a foreign country. Our men have their daily toil from morning to night, and when it is done, what do they get for it? A bit of bread and a sup of water, and sometimes little of that. . . . Let us be like soldiers' wives and stick to our colours and our banners. Never let us lose heart and give in. We have had slavery enough; we have had tyrants grinding us'.

Several women suggested that they should appeal to the queen for help.
It was said of one Quaker mining firm:

> There were plenty of the miners of the present day working for Messrs. Pease and Company who could scarce keep body and soul together; the men employed by this firm were the worst paid and most heavily oppressed of any in the county of Durham.[13]

Yet the miners offered lower levels of wage reduction and open arbitration. The latter was accepted as the way forward, and Judge Bradshaw awarded reductions of 8.75 per cent and 6.75 per cent, which both sides accepted.[14] On 21 May the men went back to work, and received a further reduction from Lord Derby of 1.25 per cent for both underground and surface workers.

In the 1880s and 1890s there were major disputes at Ushaw Moor and Silksworth. At the former village, Henry Chaytor, who was not a member of

Father Philip Fortin, the 'Pitmans' Priest'.

the DCOA, made a determined move to smash the union lodge.[15] The sacking of the union delegate on a trumped-up charge led to mass evictions, and a strike which lasted from 1881 to 1883. The local priest, Father Philip Fortin, and the President of the Catholic seminary of Ushaw College, assisted the evicted families, but eventually, by means of imported blacklegs, the strike was broken and the men forced to look elsewhere for work.

The position of the deputies caused a series of disputes between the owners and the DMA. The owners induced some deputies to form a Deputies Association, and while the majority joined it, a large number of deputies were members of the DMA. In 1876 the owners proposed higher rates of pay for the Deputies Association members, and the DMA objected, feeling that the deputies, as safety-men, should be in the miners union, and not under the control of the owners. An arbitration case, confirmed in 1881, decided that deputies in the DMA should receive the higher wage.

In 1884 the owners and the DMA agreed that the deputies should be allowed freedom to choose whether they wished to join the miners' union or remain outside. In 1890, sixty of the seventy deputies at Silksworth joined the union, but in November the lodge handed in notices as a means to bring the non-unionists into the DMA.[16] Almost immediately the remainder of the deputies joined the DMA. The lodge called off the strike, but the owners considered that the move was coercion, and Londonderry locked them out. The two sides agreed to meet, and to allow the deputies free choice. They decided on the formation of committees to discuss the question, but their meetings broke down, and Londonderry decided to evict the Silksworth men and their families from the colliery houses. These were stopped as representatives of the DMA travelled to Belfast to discuss the matter with Londonderry. He agreed to reverting to the situation as it had been prior to 22 November, when the strike started, but not to the 26th when the deputies had joined the DMA. This was unacceptable to the DMA, and at a subsequent ballot, it was decided to shut down Londonderry's Leitch, Adventure, Nicholson and Seaham Pits.

Londonderry then gave instructions that the evictions should recommence. Men from Sunderland were brought in as 'candymen', and were billeted in one of the colliery farms, while police reinforcements were moved in to Silksworth, bringing their number up to about 300. On receiving a wire, the chief constable sent his men to escort the candymen to the first street to begin the evictions.[17] The ends of the streets were sealed off, and the men began breaking open the doors, and removing peoples' possessions. After a day the candymen left, unable to stomach the task, and the company hired harder men from Leeds and Manchester. They had no compunction, and the houses were systematically cleared. Having completed their task, on Wednesday 25 February 1891, the police escorted them back to their billet at the farm, nicknamed 'Candy Hall'. A crowd, principally of women and children, followed them, heckling and clattering tin cans. Several people, however, arrived on the scene who were not local. They got into a field by the road, and began throwing stones and soil at the candymen and police.

Silksworth Colliery. Lord Londonderry's pit was sunk in 1872–3, and coal was shipped from Sunderland. By 1913 the Five-Quarter, Maudlin, Hutton, Main and Harvey were being worked by around a thousand hands.

Superintendent Oliver, in charge of the police escort, gave the orders, 'Halt, right about, charge'. [18] The constables drew batons, and ran into the crowd, flailing with their truncheons. The crowd panicked and fled, leaving about thirty people lying bleeding in the road. Several women who escaped shouted that they were unarmed, and called on their husbands to come with pick-axe handles. John Wilson, who had witnessed the scene, came up to the police line and asked for calm, and promised to clear the street of protestors. This was disastrous publicity for the owners, and they agreed to the deputies joining the DMA.

On the question of industrial relations, wages, hours and conditions generally, the DMA had sought legislation since the time of the first Gala. They complained of the slowness of Parliament to respond to their needs, and began to seek more power to influence the legislature. The Durham Miners' Political Association and the Parliamentary Committee of the TUC urged Gladstone to introduce measures for the extension of the franchise to workmen outside the boroughs. The Third Reform Act was passed in 1884, and at the general election of 1885 labour representatives, including the Durham miners' officials, William Crawford and John Wilson, were elected Liberal MPs.

There were wage rises from the summer of 1889, but the maximum realized price of coal was reached in late 1890, and then it declined. The owners met all groups of colliery workers, now united as the Durham County Mining Federation, and demanded a 10 per cent reduction or arbitration. A mines ballot rejected these proposals outright, and although there was a

John Wilson.

further offer of an immediate 7.5 per cent reduction, or a 5 per cent reduction with another 5 per cent in May,[19] this was again rejected and in March 1892 another county strike began, the greatest centres of support being in the eastern pits. Soup kitchens appeared, and suffering amongst the miners and their families increased, leading, by June, to Bishop Westcott bringing the two sides together. The miners were forced to submit to a reduction of 10 per cent.

Having been brought to its knees by the 1892 strike, the DMA joined the Miners' Federation of Great Britain (MFGB) later in the year. With continued trade difficulties generally, the owners required further reductions, but the Birmingham conference of the MFGB demanded back all reductions over the past two years, or a strike would ensue. A vote in Durham failed to reach a two-thirds majority in favour of strike action, and as a result Durham was expelled from the MFGB. [20]

Meanwhile in the political field, a number of socialist groups had been formed during the 1880s and 1890s, including the Fabian Society, the Independent Labour Party (ILP), and the Social Democratic Federation, and in 1892 Keir Hardie entered Parliament as a representative of Independent Labour. Tom Mann, who, in his early political career, had been an engineer and was later active in the 'new unionism' of 1889–91, accepted the secretaryship of the ILP, a position which he held until 1898. Later he returned to union activity and syndicalism, subjects at the heart of his speeches at the Miners' Galas of 1898 and 1899. [21]

By the time of the Boer War and a period of increased wages, the 'socialist boom' collapsed, though the fall in wages after 1900 and the threatened position of unions, particularly after the Taff Vale dispute and the House of Lords judgement, revived interest. In 1905 Keir Hardie and Philip Snowden attended the Gala, and urged the miners to change their allegiance from the Liberal party to the ILP.[22] Old Liberals, like John Wilson, did not believe that it required a distinct Labour party to deal with workers' needs, and had opposed the eight-hour movement, though this change was supported by the MFGB and the Socialists. The 1903 Lib–Lab agreement on allocation of constituencies for their candidates to fight, the 1907 agreement by Durham to rejoin the MFGB, [23] and the Federation's decision to join Labour, affected Wilson's position, though he remained until 1915 a Liberal representative of the miners in Parliament.[24]

The 1908 Eight Hours Act was to come into effect in Durham on 1 January 1910, and prior to its introduction the DMA agents reached an agreement with the owners on the operation of the Act. [25] This did not affect the hours of hewers, at seven hours ten minutes, though the putters' hours were reduced from ten to eight. The agreement did, however, remove the ten-hour time limitation on coal drawing, and the numbers of men and shifts needed for the work were to be decided by the management.

When the lodges received the details of the agreement, they reacted angrily, attacking the Executive for not consulting them. A conference of eighteen lodges at Hetton urged the county's lodges to stop work in protest over the lack of consultation, and there was a further meeting of delegates representing around 50,000 miners from ninety dissatisfied collieries in Durham City. By 14 January 1910, fifty-one pits were idle and thirty-nine were working under protest. Over 100 mines were, however, working under the new agreement. [26]

At Birtley, a group of South Moor strikers decided to try and stop men working at the new pit belonging to the Birtley Iron Company.[27] They rushed into the pit yard, straight into a trap. A force of around 100 police, armed with heavy sticks, were waiting for them. They charged, and laid about the raiders with their batons, while a second force came up behind them, and eventually chased them off.

At Murton there were three pits – a single shift pit, and the Polka and East Pits, which operated double or three shifts. In order to implement the Act, the manager proposed that three shifts of hewers and two of boys should work at the first pit, and at the Polka and East pits there should be four shifts of hewers and three of boys, where there had formerly been three of hewers and two of boys. The miners agreed to the proposals for the first pit, but not to the arrangements for the other two, and they came out in protest. Although deductions had been made from their wages for house coal, the supplies were stopped. The people, consequently, went to the pit heaps to scrape for coal, but when police reinforcements arrived, the lodge secretary appealed for calm, and the people went home.[28] As winter progressed, however, the people returned to the pit heaps seeking coal. This time hoses were

Collecting coal during the Murton strike, 1910.

turned on them, and when the police had been reinforced, they attacked with batons.[29] The crowd retreated, but picked up stones, turned, and pelted the police. They were forced to take cover behind wagons, but then renewed their attack. The people replied with a second hail of stones, but were finally forced to flee when the police charged again.

At the DMA council meeting in late January, a motion was introduced by the Dean and Chapter, Morrison, Ouston and Louisa lodges, urging the signatories of the Eight Hour agreement to resign, but when there was a vote of all lodges, the final decision was that they should be retained.[30]

Gradually lodges began to reach agreements with colliery managers on the operation of the Act at individual collieries, leaving Shotton, Horden, Murton and South Hetton still holding out. Following a mass meeting of miners it was agreed that there should be a full return to work, and the dispute ended in April 1910.[31]

In the years up to 1914 there was considerable unrest throughout Britain, amongst the railwaymen, dockers, cottonworkers and carters. In 1912, the MFGB accepted the idea of a minimum wage and came out on strike to achieve it. On 19 March the Government produced a Minimum Wages Bill, and the MFGB decided to vote on a return to work pending a settlement of rates by district boards set up under the Coal Mines (Minimum Wage) Act. Durham voted 66.6 per cent against a return.[32] The district board failed to settle the rate for the Durham district in the time alloted by the Act, and its chairman, Sir Robert Romer, made an award giving the hewers a minimum of 5s. 6d.

The outbreak of war in August 1914 saw many men enlisting for military service, though miners were classed as 'starred men' and were exempt from such duty. Yet as the slaughter on the fields of Flanders, and elsewhere, reduced Britain's forces, surface workers with their supervisors, miners of military age who had started at the pits after August 1915, and those who had lost two shifts a week over a three month period, became eligible for conscription. Tribunals were set up in urban districts to examine pleas for exemption.

In the industry there had been a gradual increase in wages. At the end of 1915, advances had raised wages 75 per cent above the 1879 basic, and in the final quarter of 1916 it was 107 per cent above.[33] The following year the MFGB sought a wage increase, and the government offered a shilling a day.[34] Sleetburn lodge called a conference of forty-four lodges and demanded raising the minimum wage and the basic by 50 per cent, threatening strike action if this was not conceded.[35] In the end the miners accepted 1s. 6d.

The same year, by orders dated 29 November 1916 and 22 February 1917, the Board of Trade implemented regulation 9G of the Defence of the Realm Act, and took control of all coalmines in the UK. A controller was appointed, but the measure did not involve nationalization, a subject which the miners had taken to their hearts.

At the end of the war, until the summer of 1920, Britain enjoyed a short post-war boom under the Coalition Government of Lloyd George, during which time the Miners' Federation urged nationalization of the mines and alterations to wages and hours. To stall a threatened strike Lloyd George set up the Sankey Commission in 1919 to look into the state of mining. The inquiry found that 'the present system of ownership and working in the coal industry stands condemned,' and to Lloyd George's chagrin, favoured nationalization and reduction of hours from eight to seven. The latter recommendation was implemented in the 1919 Coal Mines Act, and if the economic position allowed, it was hoped to reduce the hours still further to six. The Government rejected the idea of nationalization, but there was no follow-up strike. In a vote on the question of whether political or direct action should be used to achieve nationalization, the Durham miners had voted 347 for direct action and 386 for a political solution.[36]

The boom which followed the war slowed down by the middle of 1920 as British markets, particularly for established products like coal and textiles, began to recede in the wake of foreign competition. In 1920 the miners had produced about 40 million tons a year less than in 1913, and exported only 20 million tons as opposed to 73 million in 1913. The question of German reparations in coal was also a major influence on world coal prices, causing a slump in 1920–1, and later in 1925. High interest rates also affected investment in industrial operations; jobs became more difficult to find, and unemployment in the country at large had risen to 652,000 by 1920, having fallen during the war to a low point of 90,000 in 1916.

In the latter half of 1920 the nationalization question re-emerged when Robert Smillie, speaking at the Leamington conference, urged the nation in its own interest to take over production of its own coal for the benefit of the community.[37] To many this smacked of Bolshevik influence, and organizations like the People's League of London sent representatives to the coalfield to warn of the dangers of Bolshevism and nationalization.[38] The Government, however, had no intention of nationalizing the mines, and was in fact determined to decontrol them. It had also angered the miners and the general public by increasing the selling price of coal, thus massively increasing the owners' profits, while taking its own cut. The miners replied by demanding that the Government remove the increase, while seeking its own increase in wages to meet the rising cost of living. The Government refused both demands, and the MFGB voted to strike on 25 September 1920. Under the threat of bringing the full muscle of the Triple Alliance (of miners, railwaymen and transport workers) to bear on the Government, Lloyd George offered arbitration, or a scale of wage increases based on greater productivity – the so-called 'datum line' – but after negotiations the miners rejected the proposal and struck on 16 October. The threat by the NUR to close down the rail network, forced the Government to concede to miners' wage increases of 2s. for those over eighteen, 1s. for sixteen to eighteen year olds, and 9d. for those under sixteen. The miners accepted the offer.

Having been forced to make concessions to the miners, and becoming increasingly aware of economic problems, the Government proposed decontrolling the industry at the end of March 1920. The miners were stunned, for it meant the loss of all financial gain achieved under state control, and, from 1 April, a return to district bargaining and reduced wages. They therefore proposed a national standard wage, but all the owners offered was the old basic plus percentage additions paid out in 1914. The miners refused their offer and they were consequently locked out.

All coals were drawn from the pits and the ponies were brought to bank in the last days of March. Immediately Lloyd George issued an Order in Council declaring a state of emergency under the 1920 Emergency Powers Act, which allowed the Government to take control of mines, docks and railways, to use troops and to permit the police to stop and search without warrant. The Prime Minister would only allow negotiations to reconvene if the miners accepted that the Government would not subsidize the industry, and they must allow pumping to take place. As a result the NUR and the Transport Workers' Federation threatened a supportive strike if negotiations did not re-open. Lloyd George called out 70,000 military reserves to aid the civil power,[39] but in the end agreed to all sides meeting. Frank Hodges' suggestion that wage proposals might be accepted provided they were temporary and not related to a permanent settlement on a district basis, raised hopes,[40] but the MFGB executive refuted his statement and demanded a national pool. On hearing this, the NUR and the Transport Workers, who had urged negotiations, called off their support. This was 'Black Friday', but the miners decided to carry on. In Durham there was an overwhelming

Officials firing boilers at Shotton Colliery, 1921 strike.

majority in favour of the strike until the National Wage Board and Pool had been conceded, for if not, hewers' wages would be reduced from £4 2s. 8d. to £2 19s. 7d., and putters' from £3 12s. 7d. to £2 6s. 2d.[41] Boards of Guardians began to receive names of those seeking relief, and the lodges set up canteen committees to feed families. In May distress funds had been started.

After long discussion it became clear that the Government was determined to maintain the position regarding control of the industry, though it offered a series of proposals on wages. It would be willing to set up a national board, as well as district boards, to deal with wages, and these wages should include the basic plus a percentage calculated from quarterly proceeds of the district, with the provision of a subsistence wage for low paid workers. In addition, a short-term block subsidy of £10 million would be paid to aid the wage position. The miners agreed to return to work.

The economic depression continued, with increasing distress being felt by the miners and their families as pits were temporarily closed. The MFGB began to distribute food parcels to the needy, and in some areas of the county there were special efforts made to provide children with boots. In 1922 wages fell below the 89 per cent above basic, to 'starvation wages'. Not surprisingly such conditions drove many miners from the Liberal Party (which included many owners as MPs) to Labour. The Labour Party also had the support of the women, particularly after 1918; women like Connie Lewcock, an activist and member of Christabel and Emmeline Pankhurst's Women's Social and Political Union,[42] and Hannah Foster of Ushaw Moor, born in Staffordshire in 1844, whose husband was an active trade unionist who had suffered much from victimization.[43] Hannah worked for female suffrage, and in 1922, at the age of seventy-four, organized the Labour women's section that brought Joshua Ritson to the Commons as Labour representative for the Durham division.

As part of the radicalization of the pitmen, Labour MPs visited the mining villages, and at the 1923 Gala Ramsey MacDonald attended with Frank Hodges of the MFGB.

Industrially, relations were on a downward slope which was to lead to even fiercer conflict. In 1924 the miners saw the raising of the percentage above basic from 89 to 110 per cent, but in 1925, with the effects of the return to the Gold Standard, the owners sought increases in hours, even back to the eight hour day, and lower wages, while the miners resolved that there should be no alterations. In June the owners sought to terminate contracts on existing rates and to force reductions which would have resulted in miners' wages being only 8.75 per cent above those of 1914. The miners refused, and were willing to accept the owners' notices. In an attempt to save the situation the Government brought in the First Lord of the Admiralty to mediate between the two sides, but he failed. The threatened clash was, however, averted on 'Red Friday', when the Government stepped in and proposed yet another inquiry into the industry, during which period the Exchequer would provide a subvention in aid of wages up to 1 May 1926.

Portrait of A. J. Cook, from the Wingate Lodge banner. Cook was frequently portrayed on lodge banners, including those of Blackhall, Chilton, Follonsby, Hobson, Morrison, New Herrington, Philadelphia and Tanfield Lea.

The owners described the subvention as 'Danegeld' and warned that, come May, the crisis would reappear, stirred on by extremists, whom they believed to be English Soviets.

At the same time A.J. Cook of the MFGB inflamed the discontent in the pit villages of Durham. He saw the first issue of the workers as the need for a living wage, 'we will get it by reason if possible, by force if necessary. Give the miners a living wage and safety and I will give peace'.[44] The second question was control of the industry:

> 'I am convinced that at the end of the nine months the Government will be compelled, in the interests of the nation, to take over the coalmining industry, otherwise there will be a far greater conflict, because the miners will not only fight to retain their present standard, but will attempt to secure an improvement. . . .[45]

The terms of the new inquiry were announced to the national delegate conference of the Federation on 19 August 1926, and at the beginning of September Herbert Samuel was appointed chairman. His report, which appeared on 10 March 1926, advised a reorganization of the mining industry, nationalization of royalties, but a 13.5 per cent cut in wages. The miners, who had never supported the commission, rejected it. Negotiations between Government, TUC and miners, however, continued throughout April, and beyond 1 May when the subvention ended and the owners locked the miners out. On that day unions representing 3.5 million members gave their support to the miners and to a central organizing control by the TUC, but the *Daily Mail* incident on 3 May, when print workers refused to typeset an article condemning the proposed strike, was used by the government to call off negotiations and the General Strike began.

The organization of regional administration established by Baldwin became operational under the Emergency Powers Act. Commissioner Kingsley Wood took control of Durham and Northumberland. Essential supplies of food and fuel were distributed under police guard, and armoured cars were seen in Durham.[46] Some members of the public were involved in keeping services going, but in the Chopwell area miners, Labour councillors, Co-op representatives and other trade unionists proposed the formation of Councils of Action throughout the coalfield to run the strike effectively.[47] Attempts were quickly made to stop or disrupt the movement of essential supplies. County Councillor William Lawther, the checkweighman at Victoria Garesfield, who was a member of the Labour Party's National Executive, and Henry Bolton, chairman of Blaydon UDC, attempted to stop flour being moved from Winlaton Mill.[48] Both were arrested, tried, and moved under heavy guard, each to serve a month's imprisonment in Durham Jail. Steve Lawther, with Andrew Lawther and Charles Hadden, also tried to hold up food wagons in Chopwell.[49] For their efforts, they too were arrested under the Emergency Regulations, and taken to Durham Jail to serve sentences ranging up to four months, including periods of hard labour.

Horden coke-oven officials working during the 1926 strike.

Throughout these early days there was a unity of purpose in the coalfield, but in the General Council of the TUC there was concern and uncertainty about the use of the General Strike, and its direction, against a determined and fully prepared Government, particularly with the intransigence of the miners, for, as Herbert Smith of the MFGB had said, 'we've nowt to give'. In this light the Negotiating Committee decided on 12 May that it could not pursue its course, and ignominiously informed Baldwin that the strike in support of the miners would be called off. This capitulation not only seriously damaged the trade union movement, but it left the miners to fight on their own.

The levels of distress and destitution increased. As the miners were involved in an industrial dispute, they were not eligible for unemployment benefit, and many sought help from the Boards of Guardians, although single men, theoretically eligible for work, could not receive relief unless starvation had rendered them incapable. Soup kitchens began to appear in halls and chapels, along with feeding centres for children in schools. There were also social events and fund-raising schemes to provide assistance, like the *Northern Echo*'s 'Shilling Fund' and Durham City Labour Party's 'Miners' Lamp Day'.

A soup kitchen at East Hedleyhope, 1926.

At Houghton-le-Spring a supply of coal destined for officials was seized by Thomas Newton, the secretary of the local lodge, who was also a county councillor, Thomas Best, a miner and member of the UDC, and Michael Coughin, a lodge official, and taken to the childrens' feeding centre in the Miners Hall.[50] The three were later arrested and fined.

Although the lodges supported the MFGB and A.J. Cook's demand for 'Not a minute on the day, not a penny off the pay', there were indications of a small scale move back to work. By early June men at East Tanfield drift, Butterknowle, New Morley, Frankland Wood, Abbots Close and the Clink Pit at Witton Gilbert, returned on pre-stoppage rates. In July the owners made a general offer of work, with wage rates at the 89 per cent addition to basic and an eight-hour day plus one winding time for hewers. Surface workers' hours were to be the same as in 1919, before the reduction to 46.5 hours per week, without the additions to piece-rate men granted at that time, while a subsistence allowance of 6s. 8$^1/_2$d. per shift was to be paid to adult day-wage workmen. There was also a move in Parliament to increase daily hours generally to eight.

A number of mass meetings took place to protest against these moves, but on 14 July forty miners returned to the Adventure Pit at Rainton, with heavy police protection .[51] Around 4,000 miners and their families protested peacefully against the actions of the blacklegs in breaking the union's solidarity, though their feelings were expressed in the poem:

Memorial to the men who departed from this life of freedom to a state of bondage at the Adventure Pit, July 14th 1926

As Traitors we shall know them now
Because they have broke their vow
To all the rules of unity's trust,
Shout 'Baa' at them, their principles dust.

Their action now has likened them
Unto the slaves of old,
Who had to be content with work
While masters reaped the gold.

They sneak out to their toil
At night, also at morn;
Their faces are dejected, for
They are looked on now with scorn.

We hope to meet them later on
In a little smaller ring,
Where masters' rat trap promises
Will then have lost their sting.

We all bid them a last goodbye,
Their company we can spare it;
For we never want the rotten dogs
To uphold trade union merits.

So now their names are on the scroll
Of dirty blacklegs fame;
We hope their innocent children
Will recall the day with shame.[52]

A number of bishops and Free Church leaders put forward proposals to solve the stalemate, suggesting an immediate resumption of work at the old hours and wages, a government subvention to the industry for four months, with arbitration on wages if a solution had not been reached after that period, and a reorganization of the industry under the Coal Commission. The government and the owners rejected the scheme, and the miners voted 336,036 for, and 367,650 against the proposals.

Following these events, the decision to carry on was accepted in Durham, with A.J. Cook undertaking a series of visits to villages in the county. At Murton, in mid-August, he was carried shoulder high at a meeting of over 20,000 miners and their families. He asked them to stand firm, adding that, 'nobody expected Durham to do anything else'.[53]

On 17 August the National Conference of the MFGB decided that the

Officials maintaining boilers at the Hedley Pit, 1926.

executive should open negotiations with the owners for a national settlement, but the meeting two days later ended in deadlock.

An increasing number of miners consequently began to drift back to work, at Willington, Browney, North Bitchburn, Esh Winning, Silksworth and the St Hilda Pit, and the frustration of the strikers led to a number of disturbances. At Lambton Colliery the blacklegs had to be guarded by twenty police from Hull. An official of Low Beechburn lodge, who had threatened blacklegs at the end of July, received a month's imprisonment, plus a further month's hard labour.[54] A truck carrying coal from Cornsay Colliery to South Shields was attacked and overturned,[55] and at the Fanny Pit, near Gateshead, fifty blacklegs under police protection were attacked by a crowd, and several were beaten, including the company agent.[56]

On 20 October Pease and Partners offered work to their miners, and two days later thirty-seven men started at Esh Winning.[57] After the first shift the police moved the blacklegs up the main street, but Tom Clough and Sam Garr, the lodge secretary and compensation secretary, had organized a reception. They followed the strike-breakers with an improvised jazz band, while crowds jeered and booed. During the procession one of the blacklegs suddenly seized and tore up a red flag being waved by one of the onlookers, and the crowd surged forward, pushing the blackleg against a window. The police quickly moved in to get the blacklegs away to their homes.[58] Demonstrations continued, and several windows were broken.

A.J. Cook arrived and urged the men to remain loyal to the union. The colliery manager brought in police reinforcements, and they immediately arrested twenty-three of the ringleaders. Clough and Garr were each sentenced by Lanchester magistrates (who included a colliery manager) to a month's imprisonment.[59] The same day the sentences were passed, an informant warned the police that the colliery would be attacked that night. More police were drafted in, and the raid was called off.[60]

At Silksworth around seventy police were used to protect three men who went back. On 26 October, when taking the men back to their homes, sixty police baton-charged the crowd of strikers, and several people were injured in the stampede.[61] Similarly, at Ouston 'E' Pit, where the blacklegs were moved between the pit and their homes in furniture vans, the police baton-charged the pickets.[62]

At Birtley, Alexander Henry, described as a Communist, seized the offices of the Board of Guardians, with a crowd of supporters.[63] The Guardians had been dismissed and replaced by staff from the Ministry of Health, and the strikers demanded that the Ministry's ban on relief to strikers who were single men should be overturned. The office was held for nearly two hours. At Chester-le-Street, on 7 October, a crowd with bands forced their way through the gates of the workhouse to protest against the Ministry's reduction of relief from 12s. and 4s. to 8s. and 2s. 6d. Police reinforcements arrived, and as the crowd were leaving, a convoy of coal lorries under police guard passed them. One of the lorries, with police on board, knocked down and killed one of the bandsmen, but did not stop. The event was reported in the *Workers Weekly* (a London-based paper with a Communist editor, whose operations were under investigation by the Special Branch) under the headline 'Killed by scab lorry. Police brutality against procession'.[64] The official verdict on the death had been 'accidental', and the Chief Constable of Durham brought a case of criminal libel against the paper.

A number of public meetings in support of the strike were banned by the Chief Constable, including those to be addressed by Tom Mann at Houghton, and by Will Galagher, from Clydeside, at Philadelphia.

As the strike crumbled, the Government issued proposals to enable an overall return to work. It suggested a minimum percentage above basic, down to 89 per cent, a ratio for the division of net proceeds between wages and profits ranging between 87:13 and 85:15, and a subsistence allowance to low paid day-wage earners, a shilling less than it had been. It implied that there would be increases in hours, and no guarantee that all men would be reinstated. On 29 November the County Mining Federation Board ordered a ballot on the terms; the result was 40,583 for, and 49,217 against the proposals. The 8,634 majority against was not the two-thirds majority required under the rules, and the Board agreed to a return to work.

Those who did return to work before the end of the strike formed their own organizations, which became the Northumberland and Durham Miners' Non-Political Industrial Society. The society aimed at more harmonious relations between men and management. 'Peace in the coalfield is impossible so long as political extremists are allowed to do practically what they like when subsidized by the men's money', was their view, and they were determined to 'explore every avenue towards industrial peace, that work may be stabilized for some years to come'.[65] Similar unions had developed in other coalfield counties. Most developed after George Spencer, a Nottinghamshire MP on a miners' ticket, had arranged the return to work of men at the Digby Pit in October. Spencer was expelled from the MFGB conference because of it, and he developed the Miners' Industrial (Non-Political) Union to draw together the disaffected who considered that the economic reasons for the strike had been forgotten, and that the dispute was being prolonged for political reasons. The heartland of the movement was in Nottinghamshire, but it spread to South Wales, the Midlands and the Great Northern Coalfield.

The return to work was a time for retribution. Militants, lodge officials, Labour Party representatives and anyone whom colliery management objected to, for the slightest reason, were refused work. At Esh Winning Colliery the manager noted that :

> Due to the reorg[anization] after the stoppage fewer men are now required at Esh Coll[ier]y and 189 men have not been restarted. Of these 56 occupy coll[ier]y houses. At present 139 workmen are being p[ai]d rent allow[ance]. 10 notices to vac[ate] coll[ier]y ho[uses] have been served on men not now employed at the colliery and 3 evictions have taken place.[66]

The lodge officials who organized the jazz band incident were not re-employed. Clough found work as a window cleaner, but spent much of his time working for the local Labour Party, and became a county councillor and alderman. Sam Garr eventually found work at Cornsay Colliery, where he died in an explosion in 1943.

In 1928 the Plender Award reduced the 89 per cent above basic to 65 per cent, and cut 2d. from the 6s. 8½d. subsistence wage. With the trade depression, collieries began to close or be put into mothballs. Unemployment levels increased. From January to July Durham lost 10,844 mining jobs. Peter Lee, who became General Secretary of the DMA in 1930, noted that when times were good, rich owners brought large numbers of people together in employment, but when trade collapsed, they closed their mines, 'without any regard as to how the people shall live or where they shall go'.[67] The average wage per shift of a Durham miner in 1925 was 9s. 11½d., and from the 1926 strike, it fell to a low of 7s. 11½d. in 1930, remaining at around 8s. for the next five years. Taking 1932 as an example, the average wage rate was 8s. 1¼d., or an increase of 31 per cent on the 1914 wage, but this rate of increase was actually 10 per cent below the average for the British

South Hetton Lodge banner. The figure of Progress, carrying the banner of 'Emancipation of Labour,' leads the people to the 'Cooperative Commomwealth'.

coalfields. The adult subsistence wage in 1932 was 6s. 6½d. a day, which was lower than the rates in Northumberland and South Wales, but, as the miners were working short-time of around four to five days a week, his actual gross wage was only 30s. Once deductions had been made, his take-home pay came to about 26s.

Unemployment benefit of 17s., 9s. and 2s. a week was paid for a man, his wife and child, but in 1931 the Government reduced these payments by 1s. 9d. and 1s., with the child rate unaffected. Benefit was made available only up to twenty-six weeks, after which transitional payments were made, following a degrading Means Test by a Public Assistance Committee (PAC). In Durham the Labour-appointed PAC strongly opposed the practice of means testing, and in many cases gave the maximum allowance to the applicant. The Ministry of Labour's reaction was initially to warn the Durham PAC, but in November 1932 it removed the committee and replaced them with commissioners from London.[68] By 1936, seventy-three people in every thousand were seeking assistance in County Durham, compared with 25.4 for England and Wales as a whole.[69]

In April 1934 the Government appointed a committee to investigate the conditions in the economically depressed areas of Britain. Their report, which the Government was forced to publish, led to the appointment of two voluntary commissioners, one for Scotland, the other for England and Wales. The latter was Percy Malcolm Stewart, the chairman of Associated Portland Cement Manufacturers Limited. He was given responsibility for Durham and Tyneside, parts of Cumberland and South Wales. His powers were laid down in the Special Areas (Development and Improvement) Act, 1934, and the post lasted until 1937. His successor was George Masterman Gillet, formerly a secretary at the Department of Overseas Trade, and later

Parliamentary Secretary at the Ministry of Transport, who was commissioner for the following two years.

It was assumed that Stewart would have wide powers, 'to facilitate economic development and social improvement'.[70] The Act, however, clearly limited his activities, with the scheme under the general control of the Ministry of Labour, and the Special Areas Fund managed by the Treasury. The commissioner could acquire and dispose of land, with Treasury consent, give aid to projects which would provide a livelihood and independence for those involved, and give grants to local authority schemes for which there was no specific government grant. The Act, however, prevented him from giving inducements to firms to move to sites in the Special Areas, and as he found to his cost, few firms were willing to move into economically depressed areas.

Stewart favoured diversity within the local economy, and new light industries were seen as essential requirements for this change. In 1936 the Special Areas Reconstruction Association Limited was formed with Government and Bank of England backing to aid small businesses. Later in the year North East Trading Estates Limited was incorporated, and a 700-acre site was chosen at Team Valley for a new trading estate, with factories to provide work for the population of Tyneside.[71] Furthermore, in 1937 the introduction of the Special Areas (Amendment) Act saw important changes in the powers of the commissioners, particularly on the letting of factories, and the provision of financial inducements to firms willing to move to the areas. Consequently new factories were established at Pallion, near Sunderland, and at St Helen Auckland.

In 1934 the average rates charge for England and Wales was 2s. 8½d. in the pound; in Durham it was 8s. 6d., largely to cover public assistance.[72] This rating level was, in its own way, a disincentive to companies moving into the Special Area. To reduce the number of unemployed, agricultural schemes were introduced, where land was acquired and divided into plots to be worked by chosen unemployed. The scheme was largely based on keeping poultry for egg production, or pig rearing. Experiments were carried out at Mount Pleasant, Toronto and Escomb, and a piggery scheme started near the Machine Pit at Stanley, on land given by Mrs Tillard of Bath.[73]

Stewart also favoured assisted transfer, including the movement of people to the south into agricultural schemes, or as domestic servants. About thirty families were moved to Potton in Bedfordshire by the Land Settlement Association in 1934, with financial assistance from the Special Areas Fund. There was a rigorous selection process, with a formal interview, a home visit, and a training period when the men were separated from their families and sent to the new sites. The settlers were expected to grow vegetables, soft fruit, and keep hens and pigs. Some integrated, though others found that, without an assured market for their produce, they were in some cases poorer than when they had left. The Association also set up other market gardening and pig/poultry units at Andover in Hampshire, Spalding in Lincolnshire and Fen Drayton in Cambridgeshire, with settlers from Bishop Auckland,

Sunderland, West Hartlepool and a number of Durham pit villages.[74]

In 1927 Lord Durham had suggested the transfer of unemployed to the Dominions,[75] and the Ministry of Labour also favoured emigration from the deprived areas. Boys aged fifteen to eighteen were sent from Durham to Australia as new settlers, while others were shipped over to Canada to make money working at the harvest.[76] Between October 1937 and September 1938, 9,258 people were moved from the Durham/Tyneside Special Area under assisted transfer.[77]

During this period adoption schemes were also set up, to assist miners and their families and the unemployed throughout the distressed areas of Britain. During the winter of 1928, Deptford, in the east end of London, chose to select a mining village which they could personally assist. After examining candidates in the Welsh coalfield, the Mayor of Deptford, Councillor F. Ross, decided to adopt Ushaw Moor, where 600 families were considered to be in need.[78] In the thirties a Surrey-based adoption project assisted with allotments and employment schemes at Jarrow. Hertfordshire gave assistance to a pig and poultry training centre at Hardwick Hall, and provided a village hall for the people of Sacriston.[79] The Hon. Mrs Bower, also from Hertfordshire, assisted a scheme at North Hylton to train boys to work on the land. Bedford Rotary Club offered work to unemployed at the Eden Pit, the Rover Scouts in London sent money to pay for boots and daily meals for the men clearing the remains of the Tow Law Ironworks, and Sevenoaks, in Kent, provided a hall with facilities for handicrafts at Hamsteels.[80]

The level of destitution and the despair felt by a hard-working community that had seen the destruction of its principal sources of employment led to the Jarrow March, after the closure of Palmers shipyard, which the government ignored, and a series of 'hunger marches'. In the towns of Newcastle, Stockton and Sunderland, a study in 1935 found many families surviving on diets below the bare minimum laid down by the BMA's Committee on Nutrition.[81] The report also found that while in England and Wales the number of maternal deaths per thousand live births as a result of puerperal sepsis had risen from 1.57 in 1919–22 to 1.76 in 1930–3; in County Durham the number of cases had risen from 1.20 to 2.02 in the same period.[82] Puerperal sepsis and dietary deficiency were found to be connected. The work undertaken by McGonigle and Kirby in Stockton, published in 1936, also found that the death rate for unemployed was almost a third higher than the rate for employed.[83] These findings may be compared with the more recent evidence of the Black Report and the study by Professor Townsend et al. in the North East, which showed a clear link between high mortality and morbidity, and material deprivation.[84] At New Brancepeth, in 1938, a Save the Children nursery school was opened to provide for the well-being of children in the village between the ages of two and five, the first of its type in a pit village.

The discontent felt by many people led increasing numbers to move to the Labour Party, which was seen as the workers' salvation, capable of creating a just and liberal social order. The Independent Labour Party constitution aimed at 'an Industrial Commonwealth founded upon the Socialization of

Land and Capital' by 'the education of the community in the principles of socialism; the industrial and political organization of the workers, and the independent representation of socialist principle on all elected bodies'.[86]

Socialist and other left-wing literature, such as the *Daily Herald*, *The Daily Worker* and *Russia Today* circulated in the coalfield, and in some quarters there was great interest in Communism, and the achievements of the Russian Revolution. A number of lodges already had active left-wing members who agitated for social change, and their influence was to be seen

The 'Red' banner of Chopwell, with portraits of Keir Hardie, Marx and Lenin.

on the 'Red' banners of Chopwell, Follonsby and Bewicke Main. Personal contacts were established with the Soviet Union. In 1927 the children of six communists in Birtley toured Russia at the invitation of the Young Pioneers,[87] and during the 1926 strike Ann Errington, of Sacriston, went to Russia with a team seeking support for the miners and their families.[88] The leadership of the DMA was, however, strongly opposed to Communism. James Robson, the president of the DMA, spoke out against Communist activity at the unfurling of the Twizell lodge banner in July 1927:

> so far as the Communist Party are concerned, the fact was plain that members of that party sought election to miners' councils or executive committees not to obey the orders of those who elected them, but to obey the orders of Moscow.[89]

The Communist Party made a number of attempts to use the situation to forment class conflict. It also tried to take the control of miners' lodges away from the DMA and local Durham representatives, who were following a path of moderation, at Dawdon in 1929[90] and at Ryhope in 1932–3.

At Dawdon, following the Plender Award, Londonderry Collieries Limited made proposals to the lodge for cutting costs, which the lodge rejected. The DMA acquired more limited changes from the owners, and advised the lodge to accept them. Dawdon refused, and Communist influence resulted in the rejection of a further series of attempts by the DMA to reach a solution. The proposals to use the arbitration services of the Ministry of Mines, the threats by the owners to close the colliery, and the DMA to refuse strike pay if the lodge refused this arbitration, led to the strike being concluded.

At Ryhope the lodge proposed drawing cavils to decide which unemployed miners should start work when required. The owners refused to accept this scheme, and the lodge came out on strike without giving fourteen days' notice, and without DMA support.[91] On the resignation of the lodge secretary, J. Smith, who had links with the Communist Party, took his place, polling over 100 votes more than his nearest competitor.[92] When Peter Lee and James Gilliland visited Ryhope to discuss the matter they were given a hostile reception, and it became clear to the DMA leadership that this was another Communist attempt to disrupt the union. When the dispute was brought before the DMA and the DCOA, however, the lodge called off the strike.[93]

Hitler's *blitzkrieg* led to the conquest of most of Europe, and the threat of invasion of the British Isles. In Parliament Chamberlain was ousted, and a coalition led by Churchill, with Clement Attlee, the Labour leader, had taken control, to wage total war on Nazism. Though coal was essential to the war effort there was no direct Government control of the mines until 1942 when the Ministry of Fuel and Power was created. The Coal Act of 1938 had vested all coal seams of the country in the Coal Commission from 1 July 1942, and the creation of the new Ministry gave the Government the directional control of the industry, but the Government did not take financial control. Yet,

(opposite) Above, Ryhope strikers, 1932; below, police escorting blacklegs, Ryhope strike, 1932.

FIGHT FOR
BETTER WAGES
DAILY
HERALD
EVERY DAY 1

at a time of national emergency, output of coal was on the decline. In County Durham the output per man shift had fallen from 22.8 cwt in 1938 to 19.93 cwt in 1942. This was largely due to the decline in the mining labour force – a result of economic depression and migration in the twenties and thirties, and an increasing unwillingness of boys to go down the pits. Although the number of surface workers in the county had remained stable, between 1938 and 1942 the number of underground workers had fallen by about one-fifth. By 1943 Durham was looking for 5,000 workers to meet its manpower requirements.

Voluntary schemes had attempted to recruit young men to the mines, but these had largely been unsuccessful, and on 12 October 1943 the Minister of Fuel and Power, Major Lloyd George, announced to the Commons that it would be necessary to call up men for the mines as well as the armed forces. The task of recruiting extra labour was the responsibility of Ernest Bevin, who had been appointed by Churchill as Minister of Labour and National Service in September 1940. The Emergency Powers (Defence) Act of 1940, particularly regulation 58A, gave Bevin extensive powers on compulsory conscription of individuals, and he introduced a cavilling system to select recruits, based on their National Service Registration Certificate number. Those chosen, known as 'Bevin Boys', were sent to a colliery, as scheduled in the Essential Work (Coal Mining Industry) Order, 1943, where they received four weeks' training before starting regular work.

A number of schemes were also instigated to increase output. In 1943 Thomas Hornsby, Regional Controller for the Ministry of Fuel and Power, suggested a special week of extra effort should be made by different collieries in support of the Durham Light Infantry in its fight against Rommel in North Africa.[95] At Waterhouses the miners chose the week beginning 8 February as the week in which they hoped to increase output 12.20 per cent above target. At the end of the week the Union Jack flew from the pithead to mark their success.[96] Yet in Durham as a whole the county failed in every week of 1943 to achieve its output target of just over half a million tons.[97] The creation of Pit Production Committees of colliery workers' representatives and management working together to solve disputes and to increase output, improved efficiency.

In 1938 George Harvey, of Follonsby lodge, who had been one of the leading opponents of John Wilson,[98] wrote on the subject of a single union for the miners:

> . . . many Districts are troubled by the fear that the scheme, if adopted, as it stands at present, may cut across their rights and privileges now enjoyed. They are in favour of one Union with safeguards against as to local rights, and, naturally, County Unionism has bred the parochial outlook, and particularly amongst permanent officials who are, mostly, elderly men, living in the past. The rank and file should stand out boldly for one big union, for all in and about the mines, lose all narrow county views and adopt a Working Class outlook.[99]

At the beginning of January 1945 the National Union of Mineworkers (NUM) was created from the MFGB.

The efforts made in the mines and factories fuelled the war effort. The battles in North Africa were followed by the invasion of Italy, the landings in Normandy, and the unrelenting march of the Russians on Berlin. The capitulation of Germany brought Victory in Europe, and the atomic explosions in Japan saw the final close of hostilities in a world weary of war, and in ruins. In Britain a general election held in July 1945 indicated this weariness when Churchill, the war leader, was overwhelmingly defeated, and Labour took office under Clement Attlee, with the aim of creating a peaceful, caring society. Amongst its plans was its old aim of nationalization of the mines, and Emmanuel Shinwell, MP for Seaham, was given the post of Minister of Fuel and Power to carry out that aim, and to ensure that more and more coal was produced to rebuild the nation.

After the king's speech opening the new parliament, Ernest Bevin looked to the miners:

> I ask them therefore to help us, not for profit, not for the capitalists, but in the task of building peace, and bringing succour, help and warmth to millions of their fellow workers at home and abroad.[100]

Shinwell also asked Durham to increase output, and set targets at each pit.

Clement Attlee at the Miners' Gala. Attlee came and unfurled the new Brusselton Lodge banner in 1955, and his portrait appeared on the banners of Craghead, East Hetton and Sacriston.

Boldon Colliery under nationalization, 1947.

On 12 July 1946 the Coal Industry Nationalization Act received the royal assent, a victory for the miners after years of struggle. The official handing over of the industry took place on 'Vesting Day', Wednesday 1 January 1947, though a number of ceremonies took place the following Sunday. The notice boards, which were set up at every pit, read, 'This colliery is now owned by the National Coal Board on behalf of the people', and one miner commented, 'Well, they're ours now hinny'.

The 1950 Plan for Coal indicated the importance of the coastal pits to the industry in Durham, but the decreasing reserves in the west of the county, which had been heavily exploited in the past because of their high-grade coking coals, gave them a limited life-span. Consequently the inland pits generally came under increasing threat. From 1951 until October 1964, forty-four pits were closed during the Conservative administration, with the creation, in 1962, of the Inter-coalfield Transfer Scheme. The subsequent Wilson Government emphasized the need for economic fuel supplies, and the 1967 White Paper looked to other sources of energy, including imported oil, and nuclear power. Increasing research and development was being carried out in Britain in the nuclear field, which led to the Magnox, AGR and fast-breeder reactor programmes. While energy demands continued to increase, the consumption of coal declined, not only in Britain, but in western Europe and North America. During the period of Labour control, from 1964 to 1970, when the Conservatives under Edward Heath took over, colliery closures increased, with fifty-one being shut down in County Durham alone.

In 1965 national coal output was 187 million tons, seven years later it was

Bearpark Lodge banner and officials, c. 1950.

down to 138.2 million. With coal stockpiled, the miners had no leverage, and their wage position declined. In 1965 the miners had the third highest weekly earnings in British industry, but by 1970 they had fallen to twelfth place. In July 1971, a month after the election of Joe Gormley as union president, the NUM conference decided that the time had come for wages to be improved, and they put forward claims which would give face-workers £35 a week, other underground men £28 and surface workers £26, basically £5, £9 and £6 for the different classes on existing rates. The NCB offered increases of £1.80 and £1.75 for underground and surface men, which the NUM rejected. An overtime ban was started and a ballot in November decided on strike action, although, following the receipt of notices to strike, the NCB, in December and early January 1972, offered additions of 20p and 15p on their initial offer, and improvements related to productivity. The NUM rejected the offer, and the strike began on 9 January 1972. In Durham 34,200 miners came out, and pit liason committees were established to ensure supplies of coal to essential establishments, like hospitals. The miners received support from other unions, including NALGO, the T&GWU and the dockers, who had refused to unload American coal.[101]

On 9 February 1972 Edward Heath declared a state of emergency. Stockpiles of coal at Westerton were to be used for domestic purposes; the county was warned that it would be divided into blocks and a rota system introduced to avoid overloading existing power supplies and reserves of

Joe Gormley and Jack Dormond MP with the South Hetton banner.

coking coal were made available to the steelworks at Consett and Redcar. Both sides, however, agreed to an inquiry on wages, headed by Lord Wilberforce. The commission sat from 15 to 18 February, and it concluded by recommending increases of £4.50 for face men, £6 for other underground workers and £5 for those at bank. Although the National Executive of the NUM rejected these lower rates, a meeting between the miners and the Prime Minister eventually brought an agreement on 19 February, in which the Wilberforce recommendations were accepted, along with improved holiday concessions. A ballot approved acceptance, and the men returned to work on 28 February.

COMBINED EFFORTS SHALL ACCOMPLISH ALL THINGS
ASSOC. COLLIERY OVERMEN, DEPUTIES & SHOTFIRERS

NACODS officials and banner, John Street, Durham.

The increasing reliance on oil for fuel, at the expense of coal, had dramatic consequences in 1973, with the Yom Kippur War. The Israeli capture of Arab territory led to the Arab members of OPEC raising the price of oil and reducing the flow to western countries who had supported Israel. This, and the rising cost of imported foodstuffs, led to a trade deficit of £300 million in October. The level of high wage claims forced the government to accept the need for an incomes policy. A Pay Board was established, and a 7 per cent capping on wage increases, (with the possibility of 'special cases'), known as Phase Three, was introduced.

The miners refused to accept the Tory government's economic policies, and saw the oil crisis as a perfect bargaining lever for improvements in wages, while emphasizing the strategic necessity of a sound coal industry in Britain. An overtime ban was introduced on 12 November 1973, and the following day Heath again declared a state of emergency. Immediate restriction orders were placed on certain forms of heating, floodlighting and commercial displays, which were followed by the introduction of legislation to enable petrol rationing to be carried out if the situation required it. The NCB then offered a £44 million deal which was rejected by the NUM Executive.

On 28 November the Executive was called to talks at Downing Street, but the determination of the government not to allow any breach in the Phase Three policy resulted in the miners continuing the overtime ban, after the twenty-seven-man Executive voted 18:5 (4 abstensions) against acceptance of a 16.5 per cent offer.

In Durham the overtime ban, and the lack of weekend safety work, resulted in output in the last week of December being down 63,000 tons, or about 20 per cent of normal production. Limited oil supplies were being increasingly directed from industry to electricity generation, and rationing of petrol was introduced. The Electrical Power Engineers' Association refused to undertake out-of-hours repair work in late November, and in December ASLEF started a 'go slow', and agreed with the miners on a scheme of mutual support. However, after meetings with William Whitelaw, the Employment Secretary, the NCB and NUM agreed to discuss with the Pay Board the possibility of payments for 'waiting time' – the time spent in preparing for the start of the shift, and washing after it. The Pay Board refused to accept such proposals, and subsequent talks between the Government and the TUC also broke down. At the end of December the country began a three-day working week.

On 24 January 1974 the NUM Executive met to consider calling a pit head ballot on strike action. Sixteen of the twenty-seven members were in favour of a vote, including Tom Callan, the Durham Area president, and Walter Malt, the secretary.[102] The ballot, on 4 February, produced a national result of 80.99 per cent in favour of action. In Durham the result was 85.70 per cent, and the strike started on 10 February 1974.

A few days before the strike began, Heath had offered an inquiry into miners' pay in relation to other industrial workers, and the miners had agreed to put their case to the Relativities Pay Board. Their findings revealed that the miners were below the national average for manual workers, and were eligible to pay increases. However, before this was revealed, Heath called a 'who governs Britain' election. The Conservatives won 296 seats, while Labour took 301. The opposition towards the formation of a coalition government with the Liberals led to Heath's resignation, and Harold Wilson became Prime Minister on 4 March. The following day Wilson formed a Cabinet, and appointed Michael Foot as Employment Secretary. Foot immediately removed the constraints of Phase Three, and discussions resumed between the NUM and NCB. The result was a £100 million deal, giving faceworkers £45 a week, other underground men £36, and £32 for surface workers. The union accepted the offer, and returned to work on 11 March.

In 1979 Margaret Thatcher became Prime Minister. She appointed Peter Walker as Secretary of State for Energy, and the position of the coal industry, and the government's programme for its economic future, was destined to lead to a major clash with the miners' union.

At the 1980 Gala, Arthur Scargill spoke of his concern for the industry in Britain, and the possibility of major cuts in the numbers of pits and manpower:

> The Coal Board's programme will affect all areas, and Durham and the North-East are no exceptions. It is my belief that the Board's policy is to close at least 12 pits in the North- East.[103]

In April 1982 Scargill succeeded Joe Gormley as NUM president. Norman Siddall, who had had long experience of the Midlands coal industry, and had been chairman of the NCB from 1982, was replaced in the following year by Ian MacGregor. He was of Scottish descent, but had moved to America, where he became chairman of Amax Inc. In 1977 he was brought back to the UK to be chairman of British Leyland, and was then transferred to British Steel in 1980. To the miners he was seen as a 'hatchet man', come to dismember the industry. MacGregor's aim was to cut excess production, and reach a target level of saleable coal stocks. The closure of pits formed part of this plan, and the principal loss-making areas – South Wales, the North-East and Scotland – were expected to receive the first blow.

The plans for closures, with the consequent effect on employment and the mining communities, resulted in a national overtime ban, beginning on 31 October 1983. On 6 March 1984 MacGregor announced plans to cut production by 4 million tons, resulting in the closure of twenty pits, with the loss of around 20,000 jobs. On 8 March the NUM backed strikes in Yorkshire and Scotland, where there were plans to close Corton Wood and Polmaise, and offered support to any other area willing to rise up. Four days later Durham came out. Flying pickets spread from Yorkshire into the Nottinghamshire, Lancashire and Derbyshire coalfields. In London the National Recording Centre was activated at Scotland Yard in response to the heightening dispute, and police sealed off Nottinghamshire, stopping the movement of pickets. Although there were calls for a national ballot on the dispute, this was rejected by the special delegate conference at Sheffield on 19 April, and all areas were asked to support the strike.

In Durham, systems were quickly put in place within the villages, like the Hetton Emergency Committee, the Miners' Wives Support Groups and the Save Easington Area Miners campaign to organize and assist the communities through the struggle. Feeding centres were established, and donations were given towards them by Durham County Council, Easington District Council, Peterlee Town Council and others.

From the beginning pickets were sent to the gates of all the collieries, and to Philadelphia, the main NCB workshop and mining equipment store for the area. Opencast operations, like those in the Deerness Valley, Inkerman and Lumley were picketed, along with a strategic store of Polish coal in Thrislington quarry. In June, as part of a national steel blockade, strikers moved to the gates of Hartlepool and Redcar Steelworks. As much of Durham's coal was used by the CEGB, power stations were also targeted, including Hartlepool nuclear station.

Flying pickets were sent to different coalfields. Following Mick McGahey's appeal in May, miners left Durham to block coal convoys at

Pickets and police at Wearmouth Colliery during the 1984–5 strike.

Ravenscraig, and to picket Bilston Glen Colliery. In June three coachloads of Durham strikers were stopped on the road by Stoke police, but in August Durham men were outside the gates of Hem Heath, Florence, Littleton and Lea Hill Collieries in Staffordshire.

In August there were the first moves towards a return to work. On 20 August a power-loader returned at Easington, and fourteen rebels were bussed in to Wearmouth. The following day, around 800 pickets were in place at Easington, and for several days the pit was sealed off. The same day, as four more returned to Wearmouth, the picket pushed forward against the line of 350 police. The police drew truncheons, and pre-arranged snatch-squads sprang forward and grabbed twenty men, including the secretary of Blackhall lodge. The next day NACODS removed safety cover from all pits.

The police and colliery management then changed their tactics, and while 400 pickets guarded the Easington main gate, a massive police contingent took the one working miner through a back entrance. The union reacted by bussing in more pickets, and erecting blockades at the gate. Jack Dormond, the MP for Easington arrived and, after meeting Bill Stobbs, the lodge chairman, was allowed in to see the colliery manager. He advised that the situation could be defused if the worker was sent home. The manager refused, and police riot squads, with shields and helmets, were brought in to match the picket. Contact between the picket and the riot police led to stone throwing, smashed windows and batons being used. Two pickets were arrested and four police injured. Jack Dormond rushed to Team Valley to meet the area manager, as police reserves massed outside the village, but again the question of the rebel remained unchanged.

Four days later imported police reserves began sealing off the whole of Easington, preventing further pickets arriving, and refusing to allow access to all non-residents. All activity on the picket lines was filmed by police video-cameramen.

As the trickle back to work increased, a Durham Miners' Right to Work Committee was formed, apparently led by a figure known as 'Silver Birch'. Although the pickets remained solid, by October tankers had broken through the lines at Hartlepool nuclear power station, and with no strike pay and cuts to DHSS family benefit, the first two weeks of November saw increasing numbers going back. At the beginning of December the Government appointed receivers to seize the funds of the NUM. Coal began to be cut at Wearmouth, and on 2 January 1985 coal was raised at Herrington and Vane Tempest. By the middle of the month truck loads of coal were reaching the Fishburn cokeworks, and on the 4 February Lambton coke-works reopened. Finally, on 5 March the strike formally ended, and the miners marched under their banners back to the pits, and the overtime ban was called off on 2 April.

The coastal pits were still seen as economically viable, with the remaining inland sites being the main loss-makers and liable for closure. It was assumed, in July 1984, that Westoe, Dawdon, Vane Tempest-Seaham, Easington, the Hawthorn combine and Wearmouth would survive as long-life pits.[104] The Coal Board's policy on the future of North-East pits was revealed in a secret document, written up in October, and leaked to the NUM in the following month.[105] Its aim was to reduce manpower, and increase efficiency by concentrating on only four collieries – Ellington in Northumberland, and Easington, Wearmouth and Westoe in Durham – by the end of the century. Hawthorn (including Murton) and Dawdon have now closed.

CHAPTER 6

The Pit Village

Housing and Sanitation

Sinkers and miners undertaking initial development work were housed either in existing dwellings in the area, or in temporary structures, particularly wooden huts. These were either totally of wood, or with a wooden facing and inner leaf of bricks, the so-called 'Yankee style', like those at Office Row and Cross Wood Row at Trimdon Grange in the 1890s.[1]

Once the seams had been proved, and extraction began in earnest, more miners, haulage and surface workers were required, and consequently further housing had to be provided for them and their families. While there was some private housing, the vast majority of miners' houses were provided by the colliery companies. These were generally built close to the pit. There are also examples of dormitory centres in nearby villages, and within the colliery village there was often some separation of officials' houses from those of other workers.

Colliery settlements were either built on 'green field sites', or tacked on to existing rural villages. To maximize the use of available space, many mining settlements were laid out in parallel rows, like Langley Park and Wheatley Hill. At Easington, the rows built around 1900 were initially numbered in districts, such as No. 12 First Street South, though in 1926 the streets in the north, south and east sides were given names beginning with A, B and C.[2] Streets in other villages were laid out as three or four sides of a square, either around an open space, gardens, or around the colliery, as at Waterhouses, Esh Winning and Grahamsley, or else as linear or irregular plan forms, such as the disparate streets of Bowden Close – Bowden, Sebastapol and California Terraces.

Certain grades of colliery workers were traditionally provided with free houses. The number included not only officials and underground men, such as overmen, deputies and hewers, but also surface workers, like the keeker, weighmen, winding enginemen and masons. By 1925, of about 180,000 colliery houses in Britain, 68,000 were free and almost all were in Northumberland and Durham.[3]

Other working heads of families were paid a rent allowance in lieu of a free house, and where neither free house nor allowance was available, workers lived as boarders or lodgers in the houses of other workers.

The houses themselves were of stone, or, more frequently, brick. In some cases bricks from a colliery company's own brick kilns were used in house construction, each brick individually bearing the firm's stamp, emphasizing the company's ownership of the houses the miners occupied. Single and two-storied houses were provided, generally roofed with Welsh slate.

Colliery houses built in the first half of the nineteenth century tended to comprise a single room and a garret. At Reading-Room Row at Trimdon Grange, in 1892, this type of house could still be found. An investigator noted that one of the houses comprised a kitchen, containing one bed, a garret with two beds, and a small pantry, although the slates were off, and rain came in.[4] The garret had walls 4 ft high, and there was no ceiling, the room being open to the ridge, 8 ft above the floor.

Another type of house comprised two ground floor rooms – a kitchen and bedroom, and a garret. This type could be found at Thornley. They were privately built, but some were occupied by Weardale Iron and Coal Company workmen. One of these comprised an 8 ft square kitchen, with damp floor and plaster coming off the walls. The kitchen ceiling was boarded, but it was possible to see the sky through the gaps in it. A ladder led up to the garret, but no one would sleep in it. The miner, his wife and five children were forced to sleep in the ground floor bedroom.

Many of these houses also had no land drainage. In an attempt to solve the problem of dampness, several houses in South Hetton had deep sumps dug to drain water from the walls and floor, but, 'After rain these become full, and give out very unpleasant smells'.[5]

By the middle of the nineteenth century there was a move to provide

A backstreet in Ryhope.

The 'model village' of Waterhouses.

better quality housing for workmen and their families. The Peases, for instance, built model housing at Waterhouses in 1862.[6] In many improved pit villages two types of house were found in each street. The majority of the houses in the row had four rooms – a large sitting room, a back kitchen–dining-room, and two bedrooms – and were known as a 'double house'. The end houses of the rows were divided into two premises, with each unit having its own kitchen cum dining-room–sitting-room, and a bedroom. These were 'single houses'. Examples of this type of housing can still be seen at Grange Villa (1873), Low Jobs Hill, Mount Pleasant, Grahamsley and Roddymoor, near Crook, Hedley Hill, and Esh Winning.

While the majority of colliery housing had gabled roofs, some had cat-slides at the rear, which might extend down over a pantry–scullery, though it restricted height in the back bedroom. At Inkerman and Twizell the bedrooms were reached by ladder.[7] At a number of sites the dividing walls in the terrace were not built up from wall-head level to the roof apex, resulting in a continuous open attic space along the length of the street. Where a fire occurred, as at Corey Street at Ryhope on 31 May 1900, it could travel along the space, and engulf the whole street.

A number of houses in Durham villages do not seem to have been supplied with ovens. The 1842 Royal Commission on Childrens Employment found that :

> In the streets of the colliery villages are many little brick buildings used as public ovens. Small coals are put into them, and burnt until the

The Corey Street fire, Ryhope, 1900.

> ovens are thoroughly heated, and then the coals and ashes are swept out, and the bread put in, and by the heat of the bricks it is well baked.[8]

The iron kitchen range, however, supplied by firms in Durham, Newcastle and elsewhere, came to be found in colliery houses, occasionally with a round oven door, and usually with a decorative mantelpiece and metal fender. It was one of the tedious household tasks to black-lead the range. Some colliery workers received free coal, or paid for it to be carted to their home. Where house coal was supplied, the range tended to be 'banked up' with large quantities of coal, which could be raked forward as the fire burnt down.

The boiler of the kitchen range, and kettles, supplied the necessary hot water for bathing. Once the miner came off shift, he returned home grimy with coal dust. Bathing was done in a tin bath in front of the fire, usually the father first, and then sons by age. Some older pitmen would not wash their backs because they thought it would weaken them. However, in 1927, the first pit head baths were built at Boldon Colliery, and others followed. When Ben Turner, the Secretary of Mines, opened the ninety-six cubicle Whitburn baths, he said:

> There is nothing wrong with industrial dirt, only it should be left where it belongs, and these baths give the men the chance of going to work tidy and of returning home clean and happy.[9]

Families with their rescued belongings after the Corey Street fire, 1900.

Forty-eight known examples were erected in the 1950s, and the Eden baths were opened in March 1962. Of course, these baths were only for the mine workers, the women and children still had to rely on the tin bath, in some cases into the early 1960s.

Fire coal was normally stored in a brick shed, either across the back street, or in the back yard. They normally had an upper small square loading door in the back wall, and a door at the front from which the coal could be taken for daily use. Wooden boards were placed inside this door to contain the stored heap of coal. The coal delivery was normally tipped in the street, and had to be shovelled into the coalhouse by the recipient. Some villages did not have coal sheds. At Hedley Hill Over The Hill, near Tow Law, there was a track laid down the back street along which coal tubs were drawn and tipped.[10] The coal was then brought into the house and stored in a bunker in the kitchen.

The provision of water and privy facilities was often fairly basic. At South Hetton, in 1892, there were five water taps for 190 houses, and even at the model village of Waterhouses it was still necessary for water to be carried from a communal tap.[11] At settlements like Hamilton Row the water was drawn from local wells, but required boiling before use.[12] At one of the houses at Trimdon Grange, in 1892, there was a well in the centre of the kitchen. The colliery company decided to seal it up, and relaid the floor, but this resulted in dampness spreading. In the house next door a reporter found that, 'The miner was in bed when we entered. . . . All around the bed the walls were as damp as they could be. The floor was also damp'.[13]

Opening the Ryhope pit head baths, 1936.

At Trimdon Grange and Thornley, in the late nineteenth century, pit water was pumped to the surface and stored in large boilers.[14] It was then piped to the houses, and the recipient was charged 2d. per week. Further east, at villages like Ryhope, the clear water of the limestone deposits was also tapped, and supplied the whole community, though care had to be taken to avoid overworking the supply in case sea water was drawn in.[15]

The many streams and rivers of the county supplied the Durham people with water, but there were constant problems with contamination from

A household coal cart, Ryhope.

Collecting water from a communal tap, Tow Law, late nineteenth century.

human waste. The town of Darlington, for instance, took its water from the Tees, yet above the intakes, the river received drainage from twenty villages and the town of Barnard Castle. In 1890–1, in the registration district covering Darlington, Stockton and Middlesbrough, there were 2,461 cases of enteric fever in a twenty-six-week period, with 273 deaths.[16] It is not surprising, therefore, that there were moves to provide purer water, and the upper dales were called upon for it. The Weardale and Shildon Waterworks Company, which started in 1866, created reservoirs at Waskerley and Tunstall, and by 1894 was supplying 29,000 homes with clean water.[17] The provision of pure water for the population of the county was a major concern of Peter Lee, and his efforts resulted in the construction of Burnhope reservoir.[18]

The other aspect of sanitation, the provision of privies, took a long time to improve. At South Hetton, in 1842, J.R. Leifchild found no privies, only long ash heaps and dung hills between the rows of houses, and in the same village in 1892, at the 'Eight Rows', there was still only one privy for 154 houses.[19] In the same year, at Wingate, alongside new houses, there were 300 older dwellings with no privies, and this was the case with many houses in Trimdon Colliery, where huge ashpit middens lay in front of the dwellings.

With such primitive conditions, it is perhaps not surprising that in some villages enteric fever was endemic, and at Trimdon there was an outbreak of

Building new toilets, Ryhope, c.1900.

A time slate, Watt Street, Ferryhill, 1991. Similar slates can still be seen at Osborne Terrace, Leeholme.

cholera in 1854.[20] Some colliery companies did make serious attempts to solve the problem by building brick closets (or 'nettys'). One of the commonest forms of privy was the ash closet, either set up between streets, or beside the coal shed in the back yard. These were cleaned out by a scavenger under contract. The 1875 Public Health Act, and the creation of Sanitary Districts and bye-laws, tightened up on subjects like sanitation and house building.

A feature which can still be seen on some colliery houses is a slate, generally attached to the front wall. There are numerous examples in the streets of the Dean Bank area of Ferryhill. The miner chalked up on the slate the time he wanted to be woken for his shift, and a man would come round the houses to knock on his door. For the heavy sleeper, the 'knocker upper' carried a long rod, so that he could tap on the bedroom window. He was paid a few shillings by the men.

Once the miner had become old and unable to work at the pit, he was forced to leave his tied cottage, and though he might receive something from the Permanent Relief, for many the workhouse was their only prospect. In 1896 one of the great philanthropic movements of this country took root, with the aim of providing a free house and coal supply to retired miners – a 'haven of rest'. The scheme was started by Joseph Hopper, aided by Henry Wallace, Canon Moore Ede (later Dean of Worcester) and John Wilson of the DMA.[21] It brought together both colliery owners and miners to provide these things. The coal owners gave financial support, land and materials.

Sir A.F. Pease, when laying the foundation stones of eight houses at Randolph Colliery in 1924, said:

> There could be no finer work, surely, than to provide for the comfort and happiness of aged miners who had spent nearly all of their lives in daily toil in that district, and other places.[22]

The miners too contributed from their pay towards the aged miners' homes.

Although the Durham Aged Mineworkers' Homes Association began by establishing colonies in redundant colliery housing, at Haswell, Houghall and Shincliffe Bank Top, they changed to the concept of single-storied homes, either terraced or semi-detached, within the community. The homes generally comprised a bedroom, living-room–kitchen and scullery; sometimes with a front verandah on which to sit, and a lawn and back vegetable garden. A district system was also established to build and administer their homes. The district committees comprised members of the colliery unions, with a delegate to the central committee in Durham. In some cases a district might comprise a number of pits where the men had joined together to create homes for their old people. Because of the large number of delegates, meetings were usually held in the great council chamber of the DMA at Redhills, in the city.

Aged miners' colony, Cross Street, Houghall Colliery. In 1932 there were fifty-six old people at Houghall, and an institute was built for them under the Durham County Miners' Welfare Scheme. The village was abandoned in 1955.

Opening of the aged miners' homes, Ushaw Moor, 1910. Twenty homes were erected, with funds raised by the New Brancepeth, Bearpark and Ushaw Moor Lodges.

The homes were established at more than seventy sites in the Durham coalfield. Many were built in the 1920s, and even during the 1926 strike miners and owners came together to open homes for aged miners and their wives. With the Depression, the closure of collieries and the consequent decline in income from the miners' levy, the Association suffered severe financial problems. From 1939 until 1955 no homes were built, the ageing housing stock required constant maintainance, and,as a result, the Association fell into the red. It was forced to sell off some of its homes, but it became a registered housing association in 1980, enabling it to receive Housing Corporation funding.[23] The Association now has sheltered housing schemes and residential care homes, alongside its existing aged miners' cottages.

By 1901 overcrowding in the county generally had become a serious problem, and continued to be so. The 1925 Coal Commission found that:

> If, in a cottage of two large rooms and one smaller one, there were living, for example, a family of seven persons – the parents and an infant sleeping in one room, two girls in a second, and two boys in the third – this according to the English standard would be regarded statistically as a case of overcrowding. But it is certain that the family would not regard it themselves, nor would the general opinion of the locality.[24]

While some colliery companies continued to provide houses, there was a general decline in company house building. Existing stock was maintained

The Castlereagh aged miners' homes, Seaham Harbour, 1923.

by colliery craftsmen, but housing was gradually decaying, and local authorities began to take up the task of house building to alleviate the problem. Some council housing was erected following the Addison Act of 1919, and others were added under the provisions of the 1923 Housing etc. Act and the 1924 Housing (Financial Provisions) Act. To many the council house was an escape from the tied cottage and the potential threat of eviction.

As the number of colliery closures increased in later years, and people moved elsewhere in search of work, numerous villages declined. There was

Council housing at College View, Esh Winning, completed in 1923.

slum clearance of some housing, and the North Eastern Housing Association, formed by the Commissioner for Special Areas in 1935, supplied additional housing as a means to assist local authorities in their statutory duty to provide new dwellings.[25] In addition, there was the controversial classification by the county council of villages in terms of form and viability. The County Development Plan of 1951 introduced 'Category D' for the smaller villages of restricted form and limited facilities, which were expected to decline, and which were assisted to decline, by the removal of improvement grants.[26] Following the decision by British Coal in 1985 to shed its housing stock, a Durham Mineworkers' Housing Association was established to buy up blocks of housing in pit villages, and bring them up to modern standard, for the use of the community.[27] Major improvements have been made to housing in Easington through this scheme.

Women in the Pit Villages

Much has already been said about the Durham miner, but the women of the colliery villages also had a hard life. They ran their respective homes, eking out the fortnightly wage, shopping, cooking, baking, washing and bearing and bringing up children. When a husband and sons were working at the pit,

A washing-day scene in a backyard in Esh Winning.

sometimes on different shifts, the preparation of meals, and the washing and mending of pit clothes, was an almost continuous process.

Sometimes the pit clothes needed to be 'dadded' to get the dust out first. Then they were scrubbed, 'possed' in a tub with a poss-stick, and put through a mangle. The washing would be hung on a line strung across the back street, aired on a clothes-horse in front of the fire, and ironed with a flat iron. Occasionally clothes were dried in the oven if they were needed for work the next day.

Many older women recall black-leading the kitchen range, scouring the step, cooking, and baking bread and stottie cakes. Where there were girls in a family, they were required to help with the housework, sometimes staying off school on a washing day. A resident of Spennymoor recalled her childhood experiences of home life:

> I usted to greese the pit boots every night and dust the pit clothes against the wall outside also I had to go down the butchers before I went to school for meat to make me Dar a meat pudden coming in foreshift at 11 o'clock in the morning as they usted to go down at about quarter to two.[28]

Some colliery households, particularly in the late nineteenth century, employed a girl as a house servant to deal with some of the heavier tasks.

To bring in additional money, some women worked at home as dressmakers, matmakers and quilters. Frames were used in matmaking, often with old hessian sugar-bags as backing, scraps of fabric being worked in to make 'hooky' or 'proddy' mats. Larger frames were required for quilt making. The distinctive patterns used, marked up with brown paper templates, gave Durham quilting a high reputation. Payment for these items could be made gradually by taking out a 'club'. In 1932 quilted bedcovers made by miners' wives in Durham and South Wales were bought by Claridges Hotel in London.[29] Like the Hebridean crofter's wife and the Scottish fisher-girls, Durham women were also busy hand-knitters, sometimes using knitting sheaths.[30]

Beyond the home, women and girls found employment at local shops, the Co-op, as barmaids or at the pit canteens. At certain times of the year some women worked as field labourers at local farms, while others worked at the colliery, occasionally at the granary, but more frequently as office cleaners. There were thirty women undertaking these tasks at Durham collieries in 1900.[31] None were employed underground or at the surface picking-belts, though 'pit brow lasses' did work at the belts at Lancashire and Scottish pits. During both World Wars many women escaped these stereotyped roles and worked in ammunition factories.

At Seaham Colliery in the 1870s it was the rule that if a man died in the pit, his widow had a house for life.[32] If she had a son, or sons, working at the pit, that was a further guarantee of her retaining it. If the house was close to the pit, she would have to give it up if it was needed, but would be found another.

Like the men, women and children also experienced the hardships caused by industrial disputes, but the women stood side by side with their menfolk, working at the soup kitchens, tin-canning and heckling blacklegs and serving on the picket lines. In 1932 the *Ryhope Strike Bulletin* reported that:

> This strike has shown to the whole world the militant, determined, courageous, class-conscious spirit of our Ryhope women, as an active ally of the men. They have proved themselves very keen and capable comrades in maintaining the solid front, and their efforts at picketing has been wonderful; the few scabs that are working will certainly testify to that fact, and if any further evidence is needed to prove the success of our women, then we have only to look at the display of force parading the colliery and the village day and night. The changing of the guard can be seen every day in Ryhope. Why go to London ?[33]

During the 1984–5 strike the women were again on the picket lines or organizing and running the strike canteens. Miners' Wives Support Groups were established at Boldon, Burnhope, Gateshead, Sacriston, Washington and Wearmouth. In June 1984 women and children marched in force on the North Eastern Electricity Board's headquarters in Newcastle, when the Board began to cut off electricity from the homes of strikers unable to pay their bills, and forced them to restore power and arrange for payments to be made in instalments.[34] Women were also particularly involved in the picketing of the Philadelphia NCB workshops and store.

Several north-eastern women were involved in the suffragette movement, women like Connie Lewcock, and after 1918 many women joined the

Women on the picket line at Philadelphia NCB workshops during the 1984–5 strike.

Ryhope Womens' Labour Party.

women's sections of the Labour Party.[35] Their first gala, similar to the miners' annual demonstration, was held in Durham on 9 June 1923.

Food and Clothing

The sinking of pits in remote areas of the county provided the new communities with considerable problems concerning the supply of basic foodstuffs and other necessities. It is unclear what thought, if any, some colliery owners had given towards solving this. While the 'Tommy shop' was well known in some mining areas, the truck system does not seem to have been prevalent in Durham. Pedlars, with their packs containing various goods, and the hawker, with his cart, did come to supply the pioneer villages, but for some, it was a long walk to the nearest village to purchase supplies. In the early years of Waterhouses Colliery, some women used to ride in trucks on an incline railway to buy goods at Crook.[36] But, like any other frontier town, entrepreneurs soon began to appear, to supply the needs of the miner and his family. Privately built housing was erected near the rows of colliery houses, and front rooms were converted into shops. Custom-built shops were also erected, but in colliery villages these facilities came second to the Co-operative store.

The Co-operative movement began with the 'Rochdale pioneers' in 1844, and twenty years later the Co-operative Wholesale Society was formed, with its centre in Manchester. In County Durham societies were established in the 1860s, at Bishop Auckland, Birtley, Felling, Tantobie, Crook and Darlington,[37] and others followed. Some societies, in particular Crook and Annfield Plain, established numerous branches in their area. In 1872 a Co-operative Wholesale Society centre, with warehouses, was set up in Newcastle, to supply the northern Co-op stores, and a series of manufacturing works was established. Soap and flour came from Dunston; carts, wagons, furniture, clothing, drugs, baking powder and polishes from Pelaw; lard from the West Hartlepool refinery; and tin-plate from the Birtley works. By means of its purchasing depots and other production centres, goods from around the world could come to the stores of every pit village.

While generally providing food, clothing, domestic utensils, household fittings and furniture to the miner and his family, the stores also sold picks, shovels and drills for his daily work; Pelaw made miners' clothes, and Birtley the tin midgey lamps. The Pelaw works also printed many of the DMA notices and pamphlets.

The Sherburn Hill Co-op was opened in 1913, built on a base of steel and ferro-concrete because of the fissuring of the underlying limestone due to mining activity.[38] The departments there – grocery, flour store, butchering, hardware, drapery, millinery, tailoring, shoemaking and watchmaking – give some indication of the range of goods and services available in most stores

The Co-operative store, Sherburn Hill, 1913.

Crook Co-op hardware and crockery van. The Society was established in 1865 and formed branches at Waterhouses, Ushaw Moor, Stanley, Sunniside and Willington.

throughout the coalfield. The store had its own manager, with a cashier and clerks, department heads, counter staff, cobblers, tailors, apprentices, cartmen, horsekeepers and farriers.

Purchases could be made directly at the stores, or a member of the society could order and pay for goods fortnightly in the pay week. On a Monday an order man wandered the streets with a long list of goods, and each member listed his or her requirements, which were delivered the next week. This was particularly valuable for those who lived at a distance from the store. Co-op wagons pulled by two or three draughthorses travelled to outlying settlements, sometimes setting off at 9 a.m. and not returning until 7 p.m.[39] There are instances where, during severe winters, supplies from a store would be packed and sent in tubs through mine workings to connected pits that were cut off.

As a mutual benefit society, members also received 'dividend', in addition to other services offered. The amount of money spent at the store during the year, and the economic position of the store, influenced the amount of dividend received, either as a payment or entered into a share-book on 'dividend day'. The store was often the only source of food for the miner and his family during industrial disputes. The stores gave food to the soup kitchens, and goods on 'tick' to individuals, to be paid back once work resumed.

Education

The religious groups played an important part in the education of the miners' children, and there was a distinct religious element in some of their

Children and staff at Waterhouses' British School, 1899. The school was built by Joseph Pease and Partners in 1863, replacing a room in a colliery building.

teaching. The British and Foreign Schools Society, which was basically Free Church in outlook, established non-denominational schools in many mining villages. A number of colliery owners were, for various reasons, also prepared to assist, providing rooms in colliery buildings, empty houses for class-rooms, and ultimately schools, maintained by colliery craftsmen. At West Rainton the school, opened by the Marchioness of Londonderry in 1850, bore a plaque over the door which recalled that it was opened:

> As an encouragement to the colliers to promote the moral and religious education of their children, and as a lasting memorial of the interest she takes in their welfare.

Sir Bernhard Samuelson implied that he favoured a two-tier system of education when he spoke at the opening of his school at East Hedleyhope Colliery:

> If elementary schools were being built for the working population, colleges and secondary schools were also being erected for those who employed them.[40]

The colliery owners were, however, not alone in providing schools for their workmen's children; a number of companies linked to other industries were also involved with educational provision in the county. In the lead-mining industry the London Lead Company, and the Beamont-Blackett Company, provided schools in the dales, while in the iron industry, the Consett Iron Company liberally supported the British schools in its villages, and the Weardale Iron and Coal Company built Tudhoe Board School and gave the site for Tow Law National School.[41]

Up until 1891 schools charged a fee, the 'school pence', which could be a problem for some families. At Langley Park efforts were made to ease the burden on parents of large families, in 1878, when it was decided that every third brother or sister could attend free.[42]

Standards of education were laid down in the Revised Code of 1862, and provided basic knowledge of the three Rs, with needlework for the girls; additional subjects were added by the subsequent codes. Discipline was strict, and corporal punishment common.

Poor attendance seems to have been a frequent, if not constant, problem at many schools prior to compulsory education in 1880. Boys also left school in their teens to seek work at the pits. The Mines Inspection Act of 1860 required boys between the ages of ten and twelve to have a school certificate before they could be employed. The school-leaving age was raised to twelve in 1899.

The limited education received by boys before they entered the mine was a concern to the miners. It was one of the subjects of discontent raised during the Eight Hours dispute of 1910, and at the beginning of the Second World War, with the government requiring increased output, the miners refused to contemplate a reduction in the school-leaving age to bring more boys into the pits.[43] Failures in the education of children are indicated most graphically by the instances of experienced pitmen, working as officials in supervisory roles, who were unable to read or write. This was highlighted particularly when it came to the reading of the colliery rules on working practices, and to filling in the daily mine report books. At Trimdon Grange, in 1882, it was found that in one report book the entries had been written by the schoolmistress.[44] The master-shifter at Tudhoe, in the same year, was asked at the disaster inquiry if he had read any rules relating to shot-firing, the investigator adding, 'Excuse me asking you this question, but can you read ?'. The master-shifter then replied, 'Well, very little, Sir; I am not much of a reader. . .'.[45] Similarly, following the explosion at West Stanley, also in 1882, one of the deputies, 'stated that he was unable to read, and that he had never had the special rules applicable to his particular duties, read over to him'.[46]

Other miners, however, became closely involved with education. James Hoy, who started at Seaham Colliery in 1870 at the age of nine, became a member of the North Eastern District Education Committee, and was a governor of Ryhope Secondary school.[47] Hoy was also checkweighman and secretary of the Seaham lodge. John Smith, who started as a pony-driver at fifteen, and became president of the Chester Moor Lodge, was a member of the Secondary School Evening Classes Committee, and manager of Waldridge Lane and Chester Moor elementary schools.[48]

The colliery owners did make provision for adult education. Institutes were built in many villages, and were run by a committee representing the colliery management and the men. In some cases the management had a controlling interest, and some felt that the institutes were provided as a means to influence the workmen who used them. In 1907 the miners at Waterhouses Colliery secured greater control of the board of management of the institute from the management.[49] While containing rooms for meetings and playing billiards and dominoes, the institutes also had libraries and received a wide range of newspapers and periodicals. Straker and Love opened a Literary Institute at Brandon Colliery in 1873, and supplied it with 2,000 books.[50] Bell Bros. Browney Colliery reading room, and the Weardale Iron and Coal Company's library at Tudhoe each had 1,000 volumes.[51] Membership cost around a penny per week in the 1890s, and the buildings were well used. Sacriston Institute library, for example, had between 300 and 400 readers, and even the small cottage library at Framwellgate Moor Colliery had 100 members.[52] Some of the institutes, like Low Pittington (supplied by the Earl of Durham) had a lecture room for visiting speakers.[53] Pease and Partners ran art and science classes in their institutes at Waterhouses, Esh Winning and Billy Row, which were linked to South Kensington.[54] Sam Watson also established Sunday winter lectures at Redhills for miners, with speakers from the world of economics and industry.[55] A few men, like George Harvey, who became checkweighman of Follonsby lodge, studied at Ruskin College, Oxford.[56]

Medical Care

In the 1840s some collieries had agreements with individual miners to make deductions from their wages to provide for the services of a doctor. Some men gave the overman the 'doctor's money', while others hired a doctor when needed. Married men, at this time, and certainly up until 1912, paid

Waterhouses' Miners' Institute, built in 1882. It had a library, reading-room, rooms for art and science classes, and a billiard room.

6d. a fortnight 'doctor's money', while a single man paid 3d. In 1912 Lloyd George's Insurance Act was introduced, which provided for payment to doctors for medical attendance on all insured people, and the doctors formed themselves into 'panels'. At the same time, the doctors increased their charge to 9d. a fortnight, causing considerable discontent in the coalfield. At a meeting of forty-five lodges convened by the St Hilda Lodge in South Shields, it was felt that:

> The grasping greed of the medical profession makes it absolutely essential that as an organized body of workers we should definitely protect our members by taking effective steps to combat the tyranny of the Medical Association.[57]

Eleven lodges meeting at Murton decided that a county conference should be held at the Miners Hall in Durham. The subject was, however, not covered by the union's constitution, but it led some lodges to hire their own doctors. In 1918 the fee was increased to 1s.

In most villages there would be a woman who was experienced, to varying degrees, in midwifery and general nursing, and who often undertook to lay out the dead. Some colliery companies paid a woman to do this work. However, formal nursing associations were established in several villages, with funds to pay a nurse to carry out medical visits. They were run by committees, usually comprising representatives from the colliery management, lodge officials and local figures, like the minister or priest. Easington District Nursing Association, which was formed in 1919, had seventy members in 1932.[58]

Hospital treatment and care was provided at the County Hospital in Durham City, from 1853. Workmen subscribed to it, and by 1887 it had seventy-five beds. In 1902 a workmen's committee was formed, including miners, who were given representation on the governing body. Numerous lodge officials sat on the hospital workmen's committee, while others were involved in other aspects of medical care. William Cook, who became checkweighman at Pelton Fell in 1907, was a governor of Durham University's College of Medicine, and George Walker, president of Easington Lodge in the 1920s, was on the committee of Sunderland Eye Infirmary.[59]

The Religious Groups

Methodism spread into west Durham, with Wesley, himself, actively missioning to the expanding leadmining population of the dales, particularly from 1761 until 1790. By the middle of the nineteenth century Methodism had become the dominant religion in Weardale, and was widespread in the rest of the county. At the time of the 1851 Census of Worship, Methodists formed 46 per cent of all those attending services on the census day.[60] Of the 621 places of worship in the county, 351 were Methodist. Of this number, the majority, 192, were Wesleyan.

A meeting at Mow Cop in Staffordshire in 1807, influenced by the American practice of camp meetings, initiated the Primitive Methodist movement, which became a Connexion in 1812. William Clowes, and the Bourne brothers, were the leaders of this movement, and it was Clowes, himself, who established the first Primitive Methodist society in Durham, at Ingleton in 1820.[61] Although in some cases small, by 1827 thirty-eight societies had been established in the county – in Teesdale and Weardale, in several colliery villages and in the main ports. By 1851 there were 113 Primitive chapels in the county, seventy-nine less than the Wesleyans.

Methodism was organized on a system of circuits containing a number of chapels. If necessary the circuit could be sub-divided if the size and distribution of communities within the area warranted it. Preachers worked on a 'Plan', travelling to different chapels to preach, while the chapels also provided committees for running the chapel, Sunday school teachers and local preachers. Methodists were strict Sabbatarians, and opposed gambling, drinking and bad language. With the Protestant work ethic, they were particularly popular with employers. The different branches of Methodism amalgamated into a united Methodist church in 1932, but the economic depression, closure of pits, scarcity of funds, movement away of chapel adherents, and the growth of secular thinking resulted in its decline, and the closure of many chapels in the county.

The Established Church ranked second in County Durham, in terms of the number of adherents, by the mid-nineteenth century. Its provision of places of worship and clergy for the size of population was woefully inadequate. In 1700 there was an estimated population of around 95,500, with eighty parishes. In 1842 it was noted that:

> The Methodists, subdivided into variously denominated sects, have chiefly and in several instances exclusively, undertaken the charge of providing religious instruction in the collieries . . .

and that:

> It will not, therefore, excite surprise to learn that the presence of a pitman or his family in the parish church is, in most colliery neighbourhoods, a somewhat unusual occurrence.[62]

A clergyman at the time said, 'The Church should have done her duty better towards the colliers.'[63]

In 1851 there were 169 Anglican places of worship compared with 351 Methodist chapels. Some attempts were made to alleviate the problem, by dividing up the old parishes, and creating new ones to incorporate the colliery villages, particularly after 1860. These measures were, in part, the remedying of a deficiency, but it was also an attempt to combat the dominance of Nonconformity in the county. At Crook the Wesleyans attempted to hold their meetings in the village school, but the vicar of Brancepeth, whose parish included Crook, had them removed.[64] By 1910 the county population had risen to 1,402,500, with 253 parishes.

Much of the population of County Durham was still Catholic during the reign of Elizabeth I, though the failure of the 1569 rising of the northern earls, and the penal laws, took their toll on the number of adherents, though several important Catholic families survived the persecution, and retained their faith. One of these families, the Smythes of Esh and Acton Burnell, provided the land for Ushaw College, which became an important northern seminary for Catholic priests, some of whom went out to work in Durham villages. Among these priests was Aloysius Hosten from Flanders, who had studied theology at the English College in Bruges. He then moved to Ushaw College, and was ordained in 1869.[65] He worked in several Durham parishes before taking up Willington in 1877, and served as its priest for forty-six years. During his time there he built a new church, reading room and institute, and he enlarged the Catholic school. By 1851 there were twenty Catholic places of worship in the county; 3.2 per cent of all churches and chapels. The immigrant population which came to County Durham included Catholics, with an estimated 12,770 Irish Catholics attending services at the time of the 1851 Census of Worship.[66]

Members of the different religious groups in the new pit villages initially met in each others' houses or in buildings belonging to the mine company. The Primitive Methodists at Browney, in 1894, worshipped in an old wooden shed which had been a colliery store. Pease and Partners allowed their schoolrooms to be used, Wesleyans and Primitives, for instance, meeting on alternate Sundays. By means of sewing-clubs, social gatherings and street collections, the groups gradually raised money for more substantial places of worship.

The mine owners frequently supported the religious groups in their building projects, either financially or materially. Sites were either given free, or a peppercorn rent was charged, and sometimes the building materials might be supplied. Joseph Love, who was both a colliery owner and New Connexion Methodist local preacher, tended to support projects initiated by his own sect, but others were more liberal. The Quaker Pease and Fry families, for instance, contributed to all religious groups.

A variety of materials and styles were to be found throughout the county. Church and chapel layouts followed accepted forms. Anglican and Catholic churches generally had porches, naves, chancels and, occasionally, side-aisles, transepts, towers, bell turrets or flèches. Early English was a popular style. The Nonconformist chapels were generally of a simple rectangular plan, usually with a central door in the gable, flanked by lancets, sometimes with a window above, and a series of lancets in the long walls. Internally there would be a large open meeting room with pews (both public and family) flanking a central aisle, a pulpit, communion rail and organ or harmonium. A room at the side or back of the chapel would be used for meetings, temperance gatherings, Faith Suppers, or socials. In some later chapels, like the Bearpark Wesleyan, built in 1882, there is Gothic influence. The Baptist

Binchester corrugated iron chapel of ease in the 1880s. It was erected in 1876–7, and was ministered by a curate from Byers Green. The building was demolished in 1983.

chapels might also have a pool for total immersion of new members. Frequently the churches and chapels had a room or separate building for a Sunday school; at Sacriston the Primitive Methodists used a wooden partition to divide the Sunday school from the rest of the chapel.

The churches and chapels were mainly built in stone or brick. Wooden examples ranged from simple plank and plaster structures, such as St Michael's at Hett, to elaborate forms, like St Agatha's at Brandon Colliery, and St Andrew's at Ludworth, which used a framework of triangles, braced by wooden walls, the lower ends of the triangles projecting out like buttresses.[67] Wood-framed structures clad with corrugated iron were also used quite extensively by the religious groups. Several are known to have been produced in London, Liverpool and Glasgow.[68] They were comparatively cheap, but it was possible to bolt on additional sections if they were needed. Although the majority were fairly plain, the skilful use of panelling and steam-shaped woodwork, internally, could produce particularly pleasing effects. The Catholic churches at Ushaw Moor and Westwood probably reached the peak of corrugated iron church construction, with full basilican form.

Primitive Methodism, in particular, attracted working-class followers, and it played an important part in the lives of many coalminers. Following the explosion at Houghton Colliery in 1850, where twenty-five men and boys were killed, the rescuers found the body of a young lad who was known to be a member of the Primitive Methodist chapel.[69] Near him lay the burnt remains of a New Testament, which he had received from Sunday school. The organization of the circuits, with local preachers on the Plan, and the small committees established at chapels for financial matters, building maintenance, etc., formed an environment in which individual members could become involved not only in the running of their own chapels, but also in other aspects of village life – the Co-op, the lodge, and local politics. Several leading figures in the DMA were Primitive Methodists, including William Crawford and John Wilson, and some lodge representatives at Oakenshaw, Brancepeth 'A' Pit, East Hetton, Dawdon, Silksworth, Usworth, South Pelaw and Waterhouses were also local preachers and Sunday School teachers. Crawford and Wilson joined the list of coke drawers and miners who acted as lessees of a site for a Primitive Methodist chapel at New Brancepeth in 1883.[70]

While many lodge officials in the coalfield were Primitives, the other religious groups contributed to the numbers. William Jackson, the general treasurer of the Durham Colliery Mechanics, was a Wesleyan, Ernest Foster, a coke drawer who had worked with Crawford and Patterson to form the Durham Federation Board in 1878, was a Baptist, Josiah Cuttings, the Norfolk-born treasurer at Seaham, was a member of the Salvation Army, and Thomas Morley, president of the East Hetton lodge, was a Catholic.[71] Dr Towers, at St Joseph's church at Ushaw Moor, spurred the Catholics on, in 1929, when he said that:

> not only was it their duty to play their part in their trade union, but it was also their duty to participate in municipal affairs.[72]

Mine owners preferred their men to be sober and hard working. Drinking after pay-day, particularly over the weekend, resulted in loss of productivity. William Cockburn, the manager of Pease's ironstone mines, gave a rough estimate that about a sixth of his miners drank on a Sunday, and in consequence up to 25 per cent of the workforce failed to turn up at the mines on the first three days of the working week.[73] The master sinker at Bearpark wrote in his diary in 1872:

> I am sorry to report that one of the sinkers named Wm [B]ones was at the pit drunk about 9 in the morning he was interfering with the water on I ordered him away, he used very bad language and struck at me twice and struck at some of the other men he has left the place and cut, so I could not summons him.[74]

The rate of cases of drunkenness against the county population had risen from 0.849 per cent in 1869 to 2.08 per cent in 1875, with 12,045 incidents.[75] Compared with the South Wales coalfield this peak in 1875 was extremely high. In Glamorgan in the same year there had been 2,853 incidents against a population of 300,000, a rate of less than 1 per cent. Several colliery owners consequently supported the religious and temperance groups to combat the drinking problem. Numerous temperance groups had developed, particularly associated with the Non-Conformist chapels, like the Band of Hope, the International Order of Good Templars, the Sons of Temperance and the Rechabites. The Independent Order of Rechabites was formed in 1838, and by the early 1840s was considered to be 'a numerous and increasing body' in the county. It was a benefit society, but it worked for temperance and prohibition. The Order had a High Chief Ruler, with district chiefs, members, known as 'brothers', and juvenile 'tents'. For those tempted by the demon drink there were stiff financial penalties:

> If a Rechabite be convicted of having taken liquor he is fined for the first offence 5s., for the second offence 10s., for the third he is fined 15s., and if convicted a fourth time he is expelled.[76]

The Order increased its membership from the 1870s, and by 1926 James Bailey, a Primitive Methodist local preacher on the Willington circuit, and Oakenshaw lodge delegate, was Chief Ruler of 110,000 members of the Durham County Rechabites.

The Pease family actually employed temperance missionaries in their colliery villages. Thomas Rhymer, Thomas Binns and James Dack were stationed at Waterhouses Colliery, where a Temperance and Mutual Improvement Society and a Band of Hope had been formed in the late 1860s.

The career of Thomas Binns gives an indication of the background of one such missionary, and his lifelong involvement in his task.[77] Binns signed the pledge in 1839 and in 1851 began actively advocating temperance. He became a Son of Temperance in 1862 and was appointed agent for the Northern Temperance League in 1871. Ten years later he was established as a missionary at Waterhouses, and was actively involved in abstinence and prohibition movements until his death in 1897. James Dack, who succeeded Binns, was a Primitive Methodist local preacher and the last missionary in the village, dying in 1924.

James Dack, Waterhouses', temperance missionary (1846–1924).

The full membership of the groups in which these missionaries played such a leading role is not clear until the twentieth century, when the few available figures for the Primitive Methodists at Waterhouses shows thirty to forty members in the Band of Hope, and fifty to sixty adult abstainers.[78] At mass meetings, up to 300 in one week had signed the pledge, but it is not known how long the pledge lasted. It is possible that it was the strength of the temperance movement in Waterhouses which resulted in no public house being established in the village after the keeper of a small beerhouse moved to larger premises a quarter of a mile away, in the late 1860s. Apart from this, the movement did not succeed in closing down any of the pubs in the surrounding villages. By 1890 of all counties outside the Metropolitan Police District, County Durham had the second largest number of convictions for drunkenness, 10,773, which was actually a noticeable fall from the 1875 figure. Under the 1902 Licensing Act working men's clubs were also selling drink to their members. Taking the Esh and Waterhouses' club as an example, at the end of 1902 their yearly income was £3,946 4s., of which £3,780 14s. 3d. was derived from the sale of drink.[79] Yet even with this, the number of convictions for drunkenness continued to fall: by 1915 there were 3,597 cases; in 1918, 830; and in 1931 it was down to ninety-six.[80] These results may, in part, be due to the impact of the temperance groups, though the expansion of the rural police force may also have played its part.

In 1894 it was noted that:

> The miner has also a decided weakness for those prevalent and besetting evils, horse-racing and gambling.[81]

While it was always possible that a player might win, it was equally possible he might lose, and if he was a married man and he lost his wages, his wife and family suffered as well. Pitch and toss games, where the punters bet against the spinner's prediction of the coin landing as heads or tails, were held in secret locations, as were 'card schools'. Colliery managers were concerned to try to eradicate this practice. Thomas Hetton, the viewer of South Hetton, issued this notice in 1852:

> Information having been given that several of the Workmen of South Hetton and Murton Collieries are guilty of playing at Cards, and other sorts of Gambling, on the Sabbath Days; they are hereby required to take Notice, that whoever is detected doing so, will be immediately discharged and further dealt with, according to Law; and the Police have orders to watch strictly, and give the names into the Colliery Office of those who may be found acting in such un-christianlike manner.[82]

Colliery institutes also included rules against the playing of cards, and also gambling with dominoes.

Recreation

Sport has always been an important pastime amongst Durham communities. Village football teams, for instance, formed a county association in 1883, and six years later clubs from Northumberland and Durham formed an amateur Northern Football League.[83] The climax of football achievement in the Durham coalfield was when West Auckland took home the Sir Thomas Lipton Challenge Cup, considered by some to be the first World Cup.[84] This incredible team of miners won the 1908–9 season in Turin, and defeated Juventus in the 1911–12 season.

Rugby, cricket (including women's cricket teams), quoits, push-ball and hand-ball were also popular. The high walls used in hand-ball could be seen in villages like Seaham, Sacriston and East Hedleyhope and, though most have now gone, there is still one in Langley Park. At Bearpark Sir John Fry

Esh Winning winners of the Cokemens Challenge Cup, 1906–7.

opened a tennis court at the rear of the miners' institute in 1924, and the company paid a third of the cost of laying the surface.[85]

Dams set across streams provided popular bathing pools for children, but formal swimming baths were created at one or two sites. Pease and Partners opened a colliery institute at Eldon Colliery in 1912, and provided a swimming bath and gym for their workers.[86] This was probably the first industrial facility of its kind in Durham. At Dawdon colliery there was a large open-air swimming pool, with terraced seating, and warm water supplied from the colliery.

Playing quoits at Wingate Grange, 1962.

Hand-ball wall behind the Langley Park Hotel, 1991. Another example survives at New Hunwick

Music was represented by bands, male voice choirs and choral societies. Brass and silver bands 'played in' the lodge banners at the 'Big Meeting' in July, and some collieries gave financial support towards their band, supplying instruments and uniforms. The Welfare Scheme also provided loans to colliery bands. While some collieries, like Silksworth and Horden, had their own bands to lead the lodge into Durham City on Gala Day, others hired outside bands – South Hetton had the New Marske Silver Band in 1958,

Harton Colliery band, 1913.

Vane Tempest, the Head-Wrightson Band of Thornaby, Houghton had the Brampton Town Band, Wingate, the Pontefract Band, and Wearmouth, the Hammond Sauce Company Band, from Shipley.[87]

Dog racing and pigeons were, and still are, popular pastimes. Pigeon lofts, or crees, are wooden huts, with a central door and flaps, surmounted by a comb of pointed wood spars. Internally, the loft is fitted out with roosts, nesting boxes, clean water fountains and bowls. The 'pigeon man' purchases corn for the birds, and takes great care over their health, their condition after the moult, the pedigree of breeding stock etc. The homing ability of pigeons is a source of great fascination. On race day the birds are recorded, ringed and placed in sealed baskets before being transported to the site where they will be released, sometimes on the continent. A special clock is used to record the time the bird arrives back at the loft. There is always concern about the weather and birds being blown off course before they reach the loft, down at the allotment.

Most colliery houses were provided with a long garden, which served not only as a source of food, but as a testing ground for horticultural ability. Flower, vegetable and leek clubs were formed, sometimes with the colliery manager being elected as president, and annual shows were held, at least from the 1840s.

A newspaper reporter noted that:

> Every allotment and garden has its bed of leeks, and during the summer months they have been the subject of the most sedulous attention.

Mr J. Dodds' pigeon loft, Esh Winning.

From the time of planting their growth has been carefully studied and every wile known to the gardener has been brought into play to secure the best possible results.

As show time draws near the intended exhibits are the subject of jealous surveillance, for rivalry is keen and night prowlers have been known to wilfully damage the fine specimens which they feared might beat their own on the show bench.

There have been suspicions in the past that certain prizewinners were not grown in the exhibitor's own garden, that they had been 'lifted on the sly', or borrowed from friends in neighbouring districts. To prevent this, a week or two before the show, official 'stampers' go the rounds of the allotments and stamp leeks intended for exhibition.

The arrival of show day brings matters to a climax, and almost with bated breath the verdict of the jury is awaited. At the local pubs and halls long tables are set out, spread with clean paper. Thereon the exhibits are arranged to the best advantage to please the eye and satisfy the requirements of the experts.

When the judge has completed his task and his awards are open for inspection by competitors and throngs of visitors, such a hubbub of comment arises. Keen appreciation or criticism are heard on every hand, and the appraisements show how deeply versed are the critics in the mysteries of the leek culture.[88]

Commemoration of the war dead took several physical forms in the county. Scattered throughout Durham are crosses, cenotaphs and statues of soldiers,

A Ryhope gardener with his prize-winning leeks.

recording each village's loss, but the colliery owners and the miners also undertook a number of projects which served both as memorials and facilities for the community.

The first group were aged miners' homes given specifically as war memorials. Two cottages were built by Henry Stobart & Company (a Pease and Partners subsidiary) in 1924 as a memorial to the ninety-one men from Chilton Colliery who died in the Great War. Lord Joicey, also in 1924, unveiled a plaque on a single-men's hostel at Hetton Lyons, in memory of the war dead from Hetton urban district, including his son, Captain Sydney Joicey.[89]

The second group were miners' memorial halls. These were built in several villages around the county, from the Emma Colliery at Ryton to Kimblesworth. Pease and Partners lost 543 men from its mines, quarries and offices in the Great War, and at Esh Winning and Ushaw Moor collieries they gave major financial contributions towards the construction of substantial memorial halls.[90] The Esh Winning hall, built in 1923, is perhaps the most spectacular in the county, though in an old-fashioned style, principally Edwardian classicism with some examples of Art Nouveau. It is a massive work of stone, brick and terracotta, with elaborate Ionic columns at the entrance. It contained a concert hall and cinema, swimming bath and billiard room on the ground floor, and games room, library and large hall on the upper floor. The miners contributed 3d. a week towards the construction scheme. At Sacriston the memorial hall, built of brick and glazed faience, cost £12,000, towards which the Charlaw and Sacriston Coal Company gave one quarter.[91]

These halls, and many recreational projects, were assisted by the Welfare Scheme, created under Section 20 of the Mining Industry Act, 1920, which made provision for a fund, 'for such purposes connected with the social well-being, recreation and conditions of living of workers in or about coal mines . . .'[92] A penny on every ton of coal raised was taken to finance the project. The scheme was wide-ranging, from laying out cricket and football

The Esh Winning Miners' Memorial Hall, 1923. The building was opened by Mr Turner Samuels, the Labour candidate for the Barnard Castle division, and Peter Lee unveiled the memorial plaques. Today it is a grade II listed building.

grounds in many villages, constructing a swimming bath for the Lambton 'D' and Lady Anne Pit committee, to providing two nurses to work at South Hetton in 1924.[93] The scheme was transferred to the Coal Industry Social Welfare Organization in 1952.

The trend towards mass entertainment in the Victorian and Edwardian eras was seen in the pit villages, with travelling shows and entertainers. At Esh Winning, show-field entertainments came to the village, the equipment brought up by rail and transferred to the field by heavy horses. Theatres appeared, though the live acts declined as the cinema increased in popularity, and many theatres were forced to convert to this medium. At Easington, the lodge decided, in 1925, to turn part of the miners institute into a cinema.[94] It had seating for about 1,000, and was controlled by the lodge.

Workmen also began to attend working men's clubs and institutes, which appeared in the late nineteenth century.[95] The clubs were registered under the Friendly Societies Act, and had trustees, committee men, and members who paid a subscription. Such clubs were designed originally for meetings, recreation, and mental and social improvement, though from the beginning of the twentieth century they became establishments where members could drink, discuss, display leeks and vegetables at annual shows, and be entertained by acts arranged by the committee. As the clubs increased in popularity, several union lodge officials became members of club committees.

Sources of Illustrations

Jacket: front, Easington District Council (EDC), 41; back, Mrs J. Plummer.
Endpapers: front, RCA, nn; back, STC, Ind. Coal, Harton 11

The following list indicates by page number the sources and references, where relevant, for all the illustrations reproduced in the book.

5. Fillinghams, Durham
8. Author
9. Author
16. Author
17. South Tyneside Council (STC), Ind., Coal, Westoe 2
18. RCA, nn
19. RCA, U65
21. DCRO, D/MRP 9/3(vi)
22. STC, Ind., Coal, Whitburn 2
23. DCRO, D/MRP75/31
24. Durham County Museum Education Service (DCMES), 62
25. EDC, 123
26. DCRO, D/MRP42/2 (iii)
27. RCA, M247 (above)
27. Author (below)
28. RCA, M34
29. RCA, nn
30. Author
31. RCA, M251
33. RCA, nn
34. Newcastle City Library (NCL) Houghton Colliery
35. NCL, Greenside
36. NCL, Greenside
37. DCRO, D/MRP79/10
38. DCRO, D/MRP113/1
39. DCRO, D/MRP79/30
40. DCRO, D/MRP79/13
41. EDC, 41
43. DCRO, D/MRP113/1
44. NCL, Greenside
45. RCA, M82
46. DCMES, 35/16, 31

47. DCRO, D/MRP79/25
48. DCRO, D/MRP113/1
49. Author
50. DCMES, 57
51. Mrs J. Plummer
53. DCRO, D/MRP113/1
54. DCRO, D/MRP79/31
56. Author
57. NCL, Greenside
58. NCL, Greenside (above)
58. Author (below)
59. DCMES, 35/6, 25 (above)
59. Author (below)
60. DCMES, 35/6, 10
61. DCRO, D/MRP42/2 (ii)
62. Univ. Durham Special Coll., Edis B1063
63. Reproduced from Director of Horden Collieries Ltd. 1929 The Horden Collieries Ltd., County Durham, England (Darlington)
64. Author
65. Author
66. STC, Ind. Coal, Harton 11
67. Univ. Durham Special Coll., Edis H9
68. Mr W. Longstaffe (above)
68. Author (below)
69. Mr P. Hughes
70. Univ. Durham Special Coll., Edis H4
71. DCMES, 64
72. DCRO, D/MRP79/38
73. DCRO, D/MRP79/36
74. Univ. Durham Special Coll., X94, 2x2
75. DCL
76. Author
77. Mr J. Thompson
78. DCL
79. Univ. Durham Special Coll., Edis B15 (above)
79. Univ. Durham Special Coll., Edis B68 (below)
80. Mr R. Kitching
81. DCRO, D/MRP79/37
82. Mr Roger Norris
83. Mr Roger Norris
85. DCL
86. Illustrated Police Budget, 1903
87. Author
88. Author
89. *Durham Chronicle* 1/10/1880
90. Author
93. DCRO, D/X411 (16), Mr W. Moyes (above)
93. DCRO, D/X411 (16), Mr W. Moyes (below)
94. DCRO, D/X411 (3), Mr W. Moyes
95. Author
96. Author
97. DCRO, D/MRP31/2 (i) (above)
97. DCRO, D/MRP31/2 (i) (below)
98. DCRO, D/MRP31/2 (i)

99. DCRO, D/MRP40/1 (iii) (above)
99. EDC, 44 (below)
101. DCRO, D/MRP118/8, *Newcastle Chronicle & Journal*
102. Author (above)
102. Author (below)
103. RCA, M244
104. DCRO, D/PH40/6
105. DCRO, D/MRP5/3
106. Author
108. Author
109. Author
110. Author
111. Author (above)
111. Author (below)
112. Author (above)
112. Mr P. Hughes (below)
113. RCA, nn
114. Author
115. Univ. Durham Special Coll., Gibby M88
116. NUM (Durham Area)
118. DCMES, 53 (above)
118. Author (below)
120. EDC, 159
123. EDC, 61
125. Author
126. Easington, 18
127. Author
129. DCRO, D/MRP75/46, Miss J. Wade
132. Author
135. Author
137. RCA, M150 (above)
137. RCA, M147 (below)
139. Univ. Durham Special Coll., Gibby M86 (d)
140. STC, Ind. Coal, Boldon Colliery 2
141. Mr A. Crooks
142. EDC, 172
143. Univ. Durham Special Coll., Edis D4
146. *Sunderland Echo*
149. RCA, nn.
150. Author
151. RCA, U59B
152. RCA, U63
153. RCA, nn (above)
153. RCA, M259 (below)
154. DCL
155. RCA, M117 (above)
155. Author (below)
156. Houghall Agricultural College
157. DCL
158. EDC, 89 (above)
158. Author (below)
159. Author
161. *Sunderland Echo*
162. RCA, M277

163. Author
164. Author
165. Author
167. Author
171. Mr H. Henderson
173. Author
175. Mr H. Wharton (above)
175. DCRO, D/X411 (15), Mr W. Moyes (below)
176. Author (above)
176. STC, Ind. Coal, Harton 3 (below)
177. DCRO, D/Ph82/46 (75)
178. RCA, nn
179. Mr P. Hughes

References

The Durham Coalfield and the Miner

1. For a detailed account of the geology see Robson, D.A. (ed.), 1980
2. Lapsley, G.T., 1905, pp. 328, 341
3. Fraser, C.M., 1962, pp. 209–20
4. Walton, J., 1927, pp. 119–20 (D 269)
5. op. cit. p.123 (D 278)
6. Blake, J.B., 1967, pp. 1–26
7. Smith, R., 1961
8. Fordyce, W., 1860, p. 45
9. *Durham Chronicle* (DC), 25/4/1879
10. Green, J.W., 1945, p. 97
11. Parliamentary Paper (PP), 1884–5, LXXXXV, 459–63
12. DC, 28/3/1879
13. DC, 2/5/1879
14. Fordyce, W., 1860, p. 45
15. Whellan, F., 1894, p. 237
16. DC, 25/7/1925
17. Whellan, F., 1894, p. 241
18. DC, 18/7/1913
19. DC, 6/8/1897
20. Bell, W.R. & McGowan, E., 1895–6, p. 221
21. DC, 28/3/1913
22. Sturgess, R.W., 1975
23. Pattenden, D.W., 1972, p. 3–9
24. Fynes, R., 1873, pp. 82–90
25. 'To Londonderry' by John Doyle
26. Woodcock, G., 1959, pp. 3–12
27. DC, 16/5/1913
28. Wilson, A.S., 1972, pp. 90–102
29. Consett Iron Company Limited, 1893
30. DCRO, NCB 14/4, 14/6, 14/82
31. Armstrong, W.G., et al., 1864, p. 87
32. Lee, J., 1950, pp. 24–32
33. Meade, R., 1882, p. 38
34. Hollis, H.W., 1893, p. 44, 143
35. Steavenson, A.L., 1901–2, pp. 115–23
36. DC, 16/2/1872
37. Anderson, W., 1942, p. 44

38. DC, 11/4/1879
39. Wood, R., 1967, p. 75
40. Wolsingham Steel Company Limited, 1966
41. Whellan, F., 1894, p. 430
42. Bell, H., 1938–9, p. 192
43. Consett Iron Company Ltd., 1925, 12, 22
44. Johnson, R.W. & Aughton, R., 1930, p. 57
45. Political and Economic Planning Industries Group (PEP), 1936, 47
46. Williams, W.H. 1939; Heinemann, M., 1944, pp. 180,184,188,190
47. *Durham Advertiser* (DA), 27/7/1906
48. Whellan, F., 1894, p. 304
49. *The Times* 16/6/1921
50. Williams, W.H., 1939, p. 12
51. PP, 1919, XII, 143–4
52. Darlington Library, U418e PEA, acc. 34639; *Yorkshire Post*, 1/12/1902; PRO RAIL, 527/1776
53. Williams, W.H., 1939, p. 11
54. Dawdon Colliery, typescript
55. DC, 22/12/1923
56. Legge, L.G.W., 1961, p. 493; *The Times,* 23/11/1936
57. DC, 2/11/1923
58. Cousins, J.M. & Brown, R.K., 1970, p. 315
59. Garside, W.R. 1969, 5
60. DMA, 1948, 124
61. DCRO, NCB4/79
62. PEP, 1936, 47
63. PEP, 1936, 49; DC, 23/8/1935
64. DC, 16/8/1935
65. Ibid.
66. DMA, 1948, 24
67. NCB, 1978–9, 8
68. PP, 1951–2c, XII, 751
69. NCB, 1978–9, 8
70. Anon., 1960, 826–8
71. NCB, nd, 2
72. DA, 6/1/1967
73. Sill, M.,1983, p. 30
74. NCB, 1978–9, 5
75. NCB, 1982–3, 5
76. NCB, 1986–7, 4
77. NCB, 1980–81, 11; 1986–7, 4
78. The *Observer* 3/11/1991
79. Bate, R,R., Rutherford, L.A., Peart, S.D. & Cox, A.W., 1991, p. 13
80. Griffin, C.P., 1969
81. Hodges, T.M., 1969, pp. 3–18
82. DCRO, QS/OB23, 58
83. DCRO, NCB 1/JS/26(99); NCB 1/JS/28(16)
84. DCRO, D/X411/11
85. DA, 30/6/1882
86. Dodd, J.J., 1897, p. 114
87. Plaque at 62 Clyde Terrace, Spennymoor
88. PRO Census 1851, RG9/3736
89. Norris, P., 1984, p. 46
90. Emery, N., 1988, p. 156

91. Our Lady Queen of Martyrs, Newhouse, Esh Winning, Account
92. DC, 5/8/1904
93. DC, 6/6/1913
94. DCRO, D/Pe 3/46
95. DC, 1/6/1934
96. DCRO, NCB 1/TH/44 & 45
97. Charlton, W.B., 1925, pp. 87–8
98. DC, 17/10/1879; Russell Street Wesleyan chapel, Waterhouses, Register
99. DC, 6/5/1892

The Colliery

1. DC, 9/2/1872
2. DC, 25/4/1913
3. Anon., 1897–8, 97
4. Moran, L., 1988, p. 2
5. Cummings, J., 1909–10, pp. 320–1
6. DC, 17/1/1913
7. Dawdon Colliery, typescript
8. DC. 26/9/1913
9. British Coal Corporation (NE Area) nd, 1
10. Hill, A., nd
11. DC, 1/4/1910
12. PP, 1923, 174
13. DA, 27/1/1933
14. South Hetton Coal Company Limited, 1934, 6
15. NCB, Durham Div. No 1 Area, 3–4; Widdas, C.G., 1958, pp. 3–16
16. British Coal Corporation (NE Area) nd, 1
17. Anon., 1902–3b, 600–1
18. DC, 3/1/1913
19. Seymour–Wood, E., 1910, p. 229
20. Taylor, W.N., 1872, p. 73
21. Palmer, H., 1891–2, pp. 271–7
22. Anon., 1909–10, 606; Seymour-Wood, E., 1910, pp. 226–43
23. DC, 3/1/1913
24. Seymour-Wood, E., 1910, p. 231
25. Watkins, G., 1979, pp. 67–8
26. Steavenson, A.L., 1868–9, pp. 63–9
27. Anon., 1878–9, 106
28. Anon., 1906b, 4
29. DC, 1/12/1923
30. Emery, N., 1987, p. 21
31. DCRO, D/MRP 20
32. DC, 21/6/1924
33. DC, 1/7/1910
34. Mr Clarke, pers. inf.
35. PP, 1868–9, 617–8
36. PP, 1896, 517
37. PP, 1896, 516
38. DC, 21/6/1924
39. PP, 1842a, 137
40. DCRO, D/MRP 112/1
41. DC, 20/2/1926

42. DC, 16/1/1926
43. DCRO, D/MRP 11/7
44. DC, 7/10/1927
45. DA, 19/2/1932
46. Whellan, F., 1894, p. 116
47. Wood, W.O., 1900–1, pp. 189–97
48. DMA, 1938, 11
49. Whellan, F., 1894, p. 802
50. DCRO, NCB 7/5/137
51. Hall, W.F., 1883–4, pp. 37–59
52. Anon., 1902–3a, 64
53. DC, 15/6/1906
54. DC, 3/1/1913
55. Cutter set up at gates of Easington Colliery
56. British Coal Corporation (NE Area) nd, 6
57. PP, 1951–2, 934–5
58. Atkinson, G.L., 1980, p. 27
59. DA, 16/8/1957
60. DC, 5/9/1913
61. NCB, 1955, 6
62. NCB, 1955, app. II
63. Glass, R.W., 1900–1, pp. 196–201
64. Thornton, N.M., 1900–1, pp. 196–201
65. Tate, S., 1889, p. 3
66. Anon., 1902–3c, 602–4
67. Purdon, G.J., 1977, p. 14
68. Anon., 1900–1, 269
69. PP, 1842a, 168
70. DCRO, NCB, 1/Co/278
71. Stobbs, A.W., 1989, pp. 23–4
72. Gilchrist, J.R., 1902–3, pp. 572–8
73. Wood, W.O., 1894–5, pp. 42–6
74. DC, 11/8/1905
75. NCB, Durham Div. No 3 (SE Durham) Area, 3–4
76. DC, 3/1/1913; 28/3/1913
77. Teeside Chamber of Commerce 1930, 199
78. PP, 1911, 487
79. DC. 10/9/1927
80. Mr E. Watson, Ryton, pers. inf.
81. N.H.N. , 1896

Coke-Making

1. Anon., 1878–9, 105
2. Armstrong, W. et al., 1864 , p. 69
3. DCRO, NCB, 15/8(1); DC, 11/8/1905
4. *The Times,* 10/6/1908
5. Sadler, S.A., 1894–5, pp. 62–3
6. DCRO, NCB, 15/8(1).
7. PP, 1945, 27 & 47
7. Armstrong, K., 1989
8. NCB, *c.* 1958
9. Parliamentary Debates (Hansard), 6th ser., 46, 26/7/1986, 1159– 1166

Major Disasters and Miners' Safety

1. DC, 30/5/1879
2. DC, 26/8/1927
3. DA 12/8/1904
4. DA, 1/12/1911
5. DC, 22/9/1911
6. DC, 14/10/1910
7. DC, 26/10/1862
8. PP, 1923, 170
9. DC, 7/5/1897
10. DC, 27/11/1903; 11/12/1903
11. Purdon, G., nd, p. 10
12. PP, 1907, 700
13. DC, 6/6/1913
14. Engels, F., 1969, p. 272
15. Grainger, R.W. & Hurst, J.W., 1969
16. PP, 1881, 477
17. DC, 1/10/1880
18. PP, 1882a, 257
19. DC, 24/2/1882
20. PP, 1882b, 273
21. DC, 21/4/1882
22. Corser, H., 1887, p. 417
23. PP, 1907a, 691
24. DC, 19/10/1906
25. PP, 1908, 315
26. Forster, E., 1969, pp. 31, 60
27. *Consett Chronicle,* 1909
28. PP, 1942–3, 31
29. PP, 1947–8, 697
30. PP, 1951–2a, 867
31. DC, 1/6/1951
32. 'A Cross in Coal' by John Doyle
33. DC, 20/2/1926
34. DC, 22/7/1910
35. PP, 1907b, 7
36. DC, 22/7/1910
37. Lawrence, A., 1907–8, pp. 210–30
38. Spencer, J.R., 1937, pp. 78–81
39. DA, 29/8/1930
40. DA, 30/6/1944

'Unity is Strength'

1. PP, 1842, 52
2. Wilson, J., 1908, pp. 1–5
3. DC, 9/6/1876
4. DC, 29/10/1915
5. DC, 18/8/1871
6. DC, 21/6/1872
7. Moyes, W.A., 1974

8. DC, 30/7/1897
9. DC, 7/2/1879
10. DC, 21/2/1879, 4/4/1879, 11/4/1879
11. DC, 11/4/1879
12. DC, 25/4/1879
13. DC, 9/5/1879
14. DC, 9/5/1879, 16/5/1879
15. Emery, N., 1987, pp. 44–6
16. Wilson, J., 1908, p. 224
17. DC, 20/2/1891
18. DC, 27/2/1891, 25/3/1892
19. DC, 18/3/1892
20. DC, 21/7/1893, 28/7/1893, 11/8/1893, 25/8/1893
21. DA, 22/7/1898, 28/7/1899
22. DC, 4/8/1905
23. DC, 13/12/1907
24. DC, 5/6/1908
25. DC, 24/12/1909
26. DC, 14/1/1910
27. DC, 21/1/1910
28. DC, 11/3/1910
29. DC, 28/1/1910
30. DC, 28/1/1910, 11/2/1910
31. DC, 18/3/1910, 8/4/1910
32. DC, 5/4/1912
33. DC, 12/11/1915, 9/2/1917
34. Arnot, R.P., 1953, pp. 2, 171
35. DC, 28/9/1917
36. DC, 12/3/1920; *Times Weekly Ed.*, 19/3/1920
37. DC, 28/9/1917
38. DA, 17/9/1920
39. *The Times*, 9/4/1921
40. *The Times*, 14/4/1921
41. *The Times*, 5/4/1921
42. Jones, E.R., 1981, p. 55
43. DC, 26/10/1923
44. DC, 13/6/1925
45. DC, 15/8/1925
46. DC, 15/5/1926
47. Communist Party of G.B., 1965, pp. 3, 11
48. DC, 15/5/1926
49. DC, 10/7/1926
50. Ibid.
51. DC, 17/7/1926,
52. DCRO, D/MRP 127/1
53. DC, 14/8/1926
54. Ibid.
55. DC, 4/9/1926
56. DC, 11/9/1926
57. DCRO, NCB, 4/76
58. DA, 29/10/1926
59. Parliamentary Debates (*Hansard*) 5th. ser., 200, Nov.–Dec. 1926, 1344
60. DCRO, NCB, 4/76
61. DC, 30/10/1926

62. Ibid.
63. Ibid.
64. DC, 27/11/1926
65. DC, 18/12/1926
66. DCRO, NCB, 4/56
67. DC, 9/5/1930
68. Branson, N. & Heineman, M., 1971, p. 28
69. Newsom, J., 1936, p. 15
70. *The Times*, 15/11/1934
71. PP, 1936–7, 711
72. Newsom, J., 1936, p. 15
73. DC, 23/8/1935
74. PP, 1935–6, 204–9
75. Beamish Museum Archive, 4.2121.0
76. DC, 22/7/1927
77. Daysh, G.H., Symonds J.S. et al., 1953, p. 47
78. DC, 21/12/1928
79. DC, 16/8/1935
80. PP, 1935–6, 252–3; Newsom, J., 1936, pp. 93–4; DC, 23/8/1935
81. Balfour, M.I. & Drury, J.C., 1935, pp. 5–7
82. Ibid., p. 22
83. McGonigle G.E.N. & Kirby, J., 1936, p. 268
84. Department of Health and Social Security 1980; Townsend, P., Phillimor, P. and Beattie, A., 1988
85. DCRO, E/C 39; DC, 13/5/1938
86. Independent Labour Party, 1907, 71
87. DC, 7/10/1927
88. Gibb, M.H. & Callacott, M., 1974, p. 14
89. DC, 29/7/1927
90. Howard, S., 1987, pp. 3–16
91. DA, 14/10/1932
92. DA, 30/12/1932
93. DA, 3/2/1933
94. *The Economist*, 6/11/1943, 20/11/1943
95. Garside, W., 1971, p. 368
96. DA, 12/2/1943, 19/2/1943
97. *The Economist*, 6/11/1943
98. Walker, G., 1983, pp. 21–4
99. DMA, 1938, 3
100. Parliamentary Debates, 413, col. 288
101. DA, 28/1/1972
102. DA, 8/7/1974
103. DA, 18/7/1980
104. *Hartlepool Mail*, 8/7/1984
105. *Hartlepool Mail*, 19/11/1984

The Pit Village

1. DCRO, NCB, 13/366
2. DC, 23/1/1926
3. PP, 1926, 200–1
4. DCRO, NCB, 13/366
5. Ibid.

6. *Colliery Guardian*, 24/10/1863
7. Purdon G.J., 1977, p. 5
8. PP, 1842a, 144
9. DC, 31/1/1930
10. Mr V. Hindmarsh, Esh Winning, pers. comm.
11. DCRO, E/C 78, eg.10/8/1870
12. Mr R. Watkin, Hamilton Row, pers. comm.
13. DCRO, NCB, 13/366
14. Ibid.
15. Mr J. Hedley, Ryhope, pers. comm.
16. PP, 1893–4, 261
17. Whellan, F., 1894, p. 1,233
18. Lawson, J., 1978, pp. 95–104
19. DCRO, NCB, 13/366
20. Entract, J.P., 1970, pp. 9–10
21. Oxberry, J., 1924
22. DC, 12/7/1924
23. Durham Aged Mineworkers' Homes Association, 1980
24. PP, 1926, 214
25. The North East Housing Association Limited, 1960
26. Durham County Council, 1951
27. Durham Aged Mineworkers' Homes Association, 1988
28. DCRO, D/MRP3/4(i)
29. DA, 11/3/1932
30. Brears, P.C.D., 1981–2, pp. 16–40
31. PP, 1901, 127 & 508
32. DCRO, D/Lo/C626(37)
33. RCA, *Ryhope Strike Bulletin*
34. *Sunderland Echo*, 13/6/1984
35. Callacott, M., 1983, pp. 35–9; Gibb, M.H., 1983, pp. 40–1
36. Mrs O.A. Emery, Esh Winning, pers. comm.
37. Peart, E., 1970, pp. 8–21; Letch, H., 1970, pp. 46–7; Ross, T., 1911; Tantobie Co-operative Soc., 1912; Lloyd, E., 1916; Atkinson, D., 1980, pp. 5–26 & 1981, pp. 26–37
38. DC, 21/2/1913
39. Mr W. Rand, Esh Winning, pers. comm.
40. DC, 29/6/1877
41. Raistrick, A., 1977, pp. 56–66; Whellan, F., 1894, pp. 304 & 421
42. DCRO, E/NW 56
43. Arnot, R.P., 1979, 15
44. PP, 1882a, 264
45. PP, 1882b, 282
46. PP, 1882c, 331–9
47. DC, 25/9/1926
48. DC, 4/12/1926
49. DC, 22/11/1907
50. Whellan, F., 1894, p. 256
51. Ibid.
52. Ibid., p. 239
53. Ibid., p. 288.
54. Kelly & Company Limited, 1894, 46
55. DA, 18/1/1924
56. Walker, G., 1983, p. 21
57. DC, 17/1/1913
58. DA, 15/4/1932

59. DC, 11/12/1926, 2/10/1926
60. Milburn, G.E., 1974, p. 19
61. Fawcett, J.W., 1908, p. 6
62. PP, 1842b, 543
63. Ibid.
64. Lloyd, E., 1916, p. 48
65. DC, 15/12/1923
66. Smith, W.V., 1978, p. 22
67. DCRO, EP/Brd C4/1
68. Emery, N., 1990, p. 62
69. Parkinson, G., 1912, p. 53
70. DCRO, M/BDV/24
71. DC, 30/10/1926
72. DC, 31/5/1929
73. PP, 1867–8, 295
74. Beamish Museum Archive, 4.2121.55
75. PP, 1877, 661
76. PP, 1842a, 164
77. DC, 10/3/1871, 1/1/1886, 24/6/1892
78. DCRO, M/BDV2
79. Esh and Waterhouses Working Men's Club
80. PP, 1919, 349
81. Whellan, F., 1894, p. 124
82. DCRO, D/MRP 27/1
83. Hunt, B., 1989
84. Clarke, A., 1987, pp. 175–7
85. DC, 28/6/1924
86. Surtees, H.C., 1923, p. 29
87. *Sunderland Echo supplement*, 19/7/1958
88. DC, 23/9/1927
89. DC, 19/7/1924
90. DC, 3/10/1925
91. DC, 5/10/1923
92. Mining Industry Act, 1920
93. DC, 13/12/1924
94. DC, 3/10/1925
95. Ludlow, M. & Jones, L., 1867, pp. 178–9; Elkin, T., 1970

Bibliography

1. British Government Publications
House of Commons, Command Papers

1842 First Report of Commissioners for Inquiry into the Employment and Condition of Children in Mines and Manufacture, (*c*. 380), XV, 1

1842a Report on the mines in the south Durham Coalfield, between the Wear and the Tees by James Mitchell. Report and evidence of sub-commissioners; Royal Commission for Inquiry into the Employment and Condition of Children in Mines and Manufacture (*c*. 381), XVI, 1

1842b Report on the collieries, lead mines, and ironworks of Northumberland and the north of Durham by John Roby Leifchild. Report and evidence of sub-commissioners; Royal Commission for Inquiry into the Employment and Condition of Children in Mines and Manufacture (*c*. 381), XVI, 513

1867–8 Report of the Select Committee on the Sale of Intoxicating Liquor on Sunday Bill (*c*. 402), XIV, 295

1868–9 Report of the Inspector of Mines in the South Durham Inspectorate District, from 31 December 1867 to 31 December 1868, by John J. Atkinson (*c*. 4142), XIV, 613

1877 Report of the Select Committee of the House of Lords appointed to inquire into the prevalence of the habit of intemperance (*c*. 171), XI, 661

1881 Report on the explosion which occurred at the Seaham Colliery on 8 September 1880, by R.S., Wright (*c*. 2924), XXIV, 477

1882a Report of T.W. Snagge, Esq., Barrister at Law, on the explosion which occurred at Trimdon Grange Colliery on 16 February 1882, (*c*. 3319), XVII, 257

1882b Report by Arnold Morley, Esq., MP, upon the circumstances attending a fatal explosion which occurred on 18 April 1882, in the Brockwell seam of the Tudhoe Colliery, in the County of Durham (*c*. 3327), XVII, 273

1882c Report by Mr Arnold Morley MP upon an Inquiry into the Causes of a Fatal Explosion which occurred on 19 April 1882, at the West Stanley Colliery, Chester-le-Street, (*c*. 3331), XVIII, 331

1884–5 Mining and Mineral Statistics of the United Kingdom of Great Britain and Ireland for 1884 (*c*. 4430), LXXXXV, 459–63

1887 Report to the Right Honourable the Secretary of State for the Home Department on the circumstances attending a fatal explosion which occurred at the Elemore Colliery, on 2 December 1886, by Haden Corser (*c*. 5065), XVII, 417

1893–4 Report on Enteric Fever in the Tees Valley during 1890–91 by Dr Barry. Supple-

ment in continuation of the report of the Medical Officer for 1891. Public Health: 21st Annual Report of the Local Government Board (*c*. 7504), XLII, 261
1896 Report to the Right Honourable the Secretary of the Home Department on the circumstance attending an explosion which occurred at Brancepeth Colliery in the County of Durham, on 13 April 1896 by J. Edmondson Joel & R Donald Bain (*c*. 8174), XVII, 501
1901 Report of R.D. Bain, HM Inspector of Mines for the Durham District (No. 4) to HM Secretary of State, Home Department for the year 1900 (*c*. 536iii), XIV, 123
1907a Report to HM Secretary of State for the Home Department on the circumstances attending an explosion which occurred at Wingate Grange Colliery, Wingate, on 14 October 1906, by A.H. Ruegg, R.D. Bain & J.B. Atkinson, (*c*. 3379), XIII, 691
1907b Royal Commission on Mines, First Report (*c*. 3548), XIV, 7
1908 Report to the Rt. Hon. the Secretary of State for the Home Department on the circumstances attending an explosion which occurred at Washington 'Glebe' Colliery, in the County of Durham, on 20 February 1908, by J.B. Atkinson (*c*. 4183), XII, 315
1911 Minutes of evidence taken before the Royal Commission on Mines, vol. V (*c*. 5642), XXXVI, 487
1919 Return of convictions for Drunkenness in England and Wales during the years 1915–18 (*c*. 57), XLII, 349 (*c*. 360), 143
1923 Report on the causes and circumstances attending the accident which occurred in the Busty shaft of the Medomsley Colliery, Co. Durham, by H. Walker (*c*. 1965), XII, pt. 2, 170
1926 Royal Commission on the Coal Industry, 1925 (*c*. 2600), XIV, 214
1935–6 Second Report of the Commissioner for Special Areas (England & Wales) (*c*. 5090), XIII, 149
1936–7 Third Report of the Commissioner for Special Areas (England & Wales) (*c* . 5303), XII, 661
1942–3 Ministry of Fuel and Power. Murton Colliery, Durham. Report on the causes of, and circumstances attending, the explosion which occurred on 26 June 1942, at the Murton Colliery, Durham, by R. Yates (*c*. 6413), VI, 31
1947–8 Ministry of Fuel and Power. Report on the causes of, and circumstances attending, the explosion which occurred at Louisa (including Morrison Old) Colliery, Durham, on 22 August 1947, by R. Yates (*c*. 7347), XIII, 697
1951–2a Ministry of Fuel and Power. Report on the causes of, and circumstances attending, the explosion which occurred at Easington Colliery, County Durham, on 29 May 1951, by H.C.W. Roberts (*c*. 8646), XVI, 867
1951–2b Ministry of Fuel and Power. Report on the causes of, and circumstances attending, the explosion which occurred at Eppleton Colliery, Durham, on 6 July 1951, by R. Yates (*c*. 8503), XVI, 923
1951–2c Report of the Committee on National Policy for the Use of Fuel and Power Resources (*c*. 8647), XII, 751

2. Other Official Publications

DHSS Inequalities in Health: Report of a Research Working Group, 1980
Durham County Council, County Development Plan, 1951. Written analysis prepared for the County Council of Durham by W.A. Geenty
Parliamentary Debates (Hansard), Commons
Mining Industry Act, 1920, 10 & 11 Geo. V, c. 1
Ministry of Fuel and Power Durham Coalfield Regional Survey Report (Northern 'B' Region), 1945

3. *Newspapers*

Colliery Guardian
Durham Advertiser
Durham Chronicle
Hartlepool Mail
Northern Echo
Observer
Sunderland Echo, Durham Miners Gala Supplement, 19/7/1958
The Economist
The Times
The Times Weekly Edition
Yorkshire Post

4. *Durham County Record Office*

D/Lo/C626 (37)	Letter of appeal to remain in pit cottage after husband's death in Seaham explosion. E.M. Hepplewhite to Countess Vane
D/MRP 3/4 (i)	Dean Bank, Ferryhill. Letter describing various aspects of pit village life, *c.* 1920. 1976
D/MRP 11/1	Browney, Croxdale. Pit and general details of one miner's life, 1906–76
D/MRP 20	The Colliery Master's Ten Commandments
D/MRP 27/1	Poster banning gambling on the Sabbath at South Hetton and Murton collieries 1852
D/MRP 112/1	Herrington. Notes on aspects of a miner's life, *c.* 1918
D/Pe 3/46	Letter from Henry Pease to Henry Fell Pease concerning men being brought in to work in mines, 21/4/1870
D/Pe 3/130	Newspaper cuttings, the *North Star*, concerning Portsmouth *v.* Pease, 5–12/12/1900
D/Pe 3/131	Letter from John W. Pease to Walter Pease re. Portsmouth *v.* Pease, 13/12/1900
D/Pe 3/132	Letter from Lucas, Hutchinson & Meak to Walter Brunskill concerning Portsmouth *v.* Pease, Jan 1901–6/10/1902
D/Pe 3/133	Letter from Alfred E. Pease to Elizabeth Pease concerning collapse of banking business, 24/8/1902
D/Pe 3/135	Letter from A.E. Pease to Elizabeth Pease expressing hope she will be paid, 29/8/1902
D/Pe 3/141	Letter from Countess of Portsmouth to Elizabeth Pease concerning her distress at being blamed for collapse of J. & J.W. Pease, 2/10/1902
D/Pe 3/142	Letter from Elizabeth Pease to Countess of Portsmouth concerning details in Portsmouth *v.* Pease, 29/10/1902
D/Pe 3/145	Extracts from J.A. Pease's papers re. circumstances leading to the bank collapse, *c.* 1902
D/Pe 3/146	Note on amount owing and lost, *c.* 1902
D/X411/11	Wingate Grange Colliery. Agreement with miners from Cornwall, 1866–76
E/C 78	Waterhouses British school log-book
E/NW 56	Langley Park school log-book
EP/Brd C41	Plan and elevations of the church of St Agatha, Brandon Colliery
M/BDV 2	Waterhouses Primitive Methodist circuit, circuit reports, schedules of Sunday schools, 1893–1932
M/BDV 24	Brandon and Deerness valley circuit. Property schedules
NCB 1/JS/26(99)	Papers of John Bell Simpson. Correspondence, T. Cowden, Cumberland, 1866

CB 1/JS/28(16)	J. Harrison re. Stargate and Emma Pit, and employment of Fletcher, from Cumberland, 1866
NCB 1/TH/44	Papers of Thomas Hall Young. Agreement for hiring and service of workmen, 1840
NCB 1/TH/45	Agreement by workmen for making allowances to wives, 1840
NCB 4/56	Pease and Partners manager's rough notes, 1926-8
NCB 7/5/137	Correspondence, agreements and papers re. pneumatic pick dispute at Beamish Colliery, 28/12/1934–19/6/1936
NCB 13/366	Newspaper cuttings on 'The Homes of the Pitmen', Sept. to Nov. 1892
NCB 14/4	Declaration of trust, 25/10/1850
NCB 14/6	Declaration of trust, 5/10/1852
NCB 14/82	Copy and covenant for sale and purchase of coal from Viscount Boynes Thornley Pit House estate
NCB 15/8(1)	DCOA and Durham Cokemen's Assoc. Joint returns as to by-product ovens, Feb. 1907
QS/OB23, 58	Quarter Sessions Order Book, April 1854–Dec. 1859

5. Other Primary Sources

Beamish Museum Archive
4.2121.0 Letter from Lord Lambton to the Mayor of Gateshead 11/1/1927
4.2121.55 Diary of the sinking of Bearpark Colliery

Darlington Library
U418e PEA acc. 34639. An historical outline of the association of Edward Pease, Joseph Pease and Joseph Whitwell Pease

Dawdon Colliery Office
'Dawdon Colliery. Seaham Harbour. February 1908', typescript report of sinking

Esh and Waterhouses Working Men's Club
Annual return for the year ending 31/12/1902

Labour Party (Walworth Rd, London)
ILP Annual Report 1907

Our Lady Queen of Martyrs, Newhouse, Esh Winning
Account for Distress Fund

Public Record Office
Census 1851, RG9/3736
Rail 527/1776, Resignation of J.W. Pease from chairmanship of North Eastern Railway Company

Ryhope Community Association
Ryhope Strike Bulletin, 1932

Russell Street Wesleyan Methodist Church
Waterhouses Sunday school attendance register

6. *Books and Articles*

Place of publication is given only if outside London

Anderson, W., 'Ironstones in North East England', in Caesar, A. A.L., 1942, pp. 43–5

Anon.,'Visit to Browney Colliery', North of England Institute of Mining and Mechanical Engineers NEIMME, XXVIII, 1878–9, pp. 105–6

Anon., 'Whitburn Colliery', *Transactions of the Institute of Mining Engineers* TIME, XVIII, 1897–8, pp. 97–8

Anon.,'Bearpark Colliery' TIME, XXI, 1900–1, pp. 269

Anon., ' Newbottle Colleries' NEIMME, XXIV, 1902–1,pp. 63–6

Anon., ' Dawdon Colliery' TIME, XXIV, 1902–3b, pp 600–1

Anon., ''Hylton Colliery' TIME, XXIV, 1902–3c, pp. 602–4

Anon., ' Dawdon Colliery' NEIMME, XXXII, 1906a, pp 2–4

Anon., 'Horden Collieries' NEIMME, XXXII, 1906b, pp. 4–5

Anon., 'The Harton Coal Company Limited' TIME, XXXVIII, 1909–10, pp. 605–11

Anon., 'Consett Iron Company Limited – A Technical Survey', *Iron & Coal Trades Review* , CLXVIII, no. 4481A, 1954, pp. 10–13

Anon., 'Hawthorn Combined Mine', *The Engineer* 210, no. 5469, 1960, pp. 826–8

Armstrong, K., *From Fissebourne to Fishburn*. Durham, 1989

Armstrong, W.G. et al., *The Industrial Resources of the Tyne, Wear and Tees*. 1864

Arnot, R.P., *The Miners*. 1953 and 1979

Atkinson, D., 'Co-operation in Darlington 1868–1900', Durham Co. Local Hist. Soc. 25, 1980, pp. 5–26

Balfour, M.I. & Drury, J.C., *Motherhood in the Special Areas of Durham and Tyneside*. 1935

Bate, R.R., Rutherford, L.A., Peart, S.D. & Cox, A.W., *Campaigners' Guide to Opencast Coal Mining*. 1991

Bell, H., 'A brief history of the Consett Iron Company Limited', *Durham Univ. Journal*, 31, 1938–9, pp. 190–3

Bell, W.R. & McGowan, E., 'Haulage at Wearmouth Colliery', TIME, XI, 1895–6, pp. 221–6

Blake, J. B., ' The medieval coal trade of North East England: some fourteenth-century evidence *Northern History*, 2, 1967, pp. 1–26

Branson, N. & Heinemann, M., *Britain in the Nineteen thirties*. 1971

Brears, P.C.D., 'The knitting sheath', *Folk Life*, 20, 1981–2, pp. 16–40

British Coal Corporation, North East Area and Dawdon Colliery (nl)

Bulmer, M., *Mining and Social Change*. 1978

Caesar, A.A.L., *A Survey of Industrial Facilities of the North East Region*. Newcastle, 1942

Callacott, M., 'Labour women in North-East England', *North East Labour History*, 17, 1983, pp. 35–9

Charlton, W.B., *A Fifty Years' History of the Durham County Colliery Enginemen's, Boiler-Minders' and Firemen's Association*. Durham, 1925

Clarke, A., 'The Sir Thomas Lipton Football Challenge Trophy', *FA Yearbook*, 1987, pp. 175–7

Consett Chronicle, *The Consett Chronicle memento of the lamentable colliery disaster at West Stanley*. Consett,1909

Consett Iron Company Limited, *Description of the Works* . Newcastle, 1893

——, *Consett Iron Co. Limited*. Leeds, 1925

Cousins, J.M. & Brown, R.K., 'Shipbuilding', in Dewdney, J.C., 1970, pp. 313–29

Cummings, J., 'Sinking of the John shaft at Hamsterley Colliery through sand and gravel by means of underhanging tubbing', NEIMME, XXXVIII, 1909–10, pp. 320–31

Darby, J.H., 'The Semet-Solvay coke oven', TIME, IX, 1894–5, pp. 54–68

Daysh, G.H., Symonds J.S. et al., *West Durham: A Study of a Problem Area in North Eastern England*. Oxford, 1953

Dewdney, J.C., *Durham County and City with Teeside*. Durham, 1970
DMA, *Durham Miners Monthly Journal*, 8, 1938
——, *Annual Gala Souvenir*. Durham, 1948
Dodd, J.J., *The History of the Urban District of Spennymoor*. Spennymoor, 1897
Durham Aged Mineworkers Homes Association, *Eighty-first Annual Report*. Durham, 1980
Durham Mineworker's Homes Association, *Second Annual Report*. Durham, 1988
Elkin, T., *So they brewed their own beer. A History of the Northern Clubs and Federation Brewery Ltd*. Newcastle, 1970
Emery, N., 'The Ushaw Moor miners strike and evictions, 1881–3', *North East Labour History*, 21, 1987, pp. 44–6
——, *The Deerness Valley: A History of Settlement in a Durham Valley*. Durham Univ. Dept. of Archaeology Occ. Paper 9, 1988
——, 'Corrugated iron public buildings in County Durham', *Durham Archaeological Journal* 6, 1990, pp. 59–73
Engels, F., (ed.), *The Condition of the Working Class in England*. 1969
Entract, J.P., ' "Chlorodyne" Browne', *London Hospital Gazette*, LXXIII, 4, 1970, pp. 7–11
Fawcett, J.W., *Memorials of Early Primitive Methodism in the County of Durham, 1820–1829*. Durham, 1908
Fordyce, W., *A History of Coal, Coke, Coalfields and Iron Manufacture in Northern England*. Newcastle, 1860. (Reprinted 1973)
Forster, E., *The Death Pit: The story of the West Stanley colliery explosion 1909*. Newcastle, 1969
Fraser, C.M., 'The North East coal trade until 1421', *Trans D & N*, 4 ser, XI, 1962, pp. 209–20
Fynes, R., *History of Northumberland and Durham Miners*. Sunderland, 1873. (Reprinted 1923)
Garside, W.R., 'The North-Eastern Coalfield and the Export Trade, 1919–39', *DUJ*, LXII, 1969, pp. 1–15
——, *The Durham Miners 1919–1960*. 1971
Gibb, M.H., 'The first Durham Labour Women's Gala', *North East Labour History* 17, 1983, pp. 40–1
Gibb, M.H., & Callacott, M., 'The Labour Party in the North East between the Wars', *North East Labour History* 8, 1974, pp. 9–15
Gilchrist, J.R., 'Garesfield railway and incline', NEIMME, XXIV, 1902–3, pp. 572–8
Grainger, R.W. & Hurst, J.W., *A report on the incidence of disability amongst Durham miners*. Durham Univ. Dept. of Economics, 1969
Green, J.W., 'Notes on geology of Claypath Crossing' in Sharp, T. 1945, pp. 96–8
Gregory, J. & Stobbs, J.T., 'Notes on the Koepe system of winding', TIME, XVIII, 1900, pp. 450–7
Glass, R.W., 'Endless–rope haulage at Axwell Park Colliery', TIME, XXI, 1900–1, pp. 167–73
Hall, W.F., 'The Haswell mechanical coal getter: an invention for working coal without the aid of gunpowder or other explosives', NEIMME, XXXIII, 1883–4, pp. 37–59
Heinemann, M., *Britain's Coal: A Study of the Mining Crisis*. 1944
Hill, A., *Single cylinder vertical lever type winding engines as used in the North East of England*. Eindhoven
Hodges, T.M., 'The Peopling of the Hinterland and Port of Cardiff, 1801–1914', in Minchin, W.E., (ed.), 1969, pp. 3–18
Hollis, H.W., 'The Tudhoe works of the Weardale Iron and Coal Co. Ltd.', *Journal of the Iron & Steel Institute*, 44, 1893, pp. 142–54
Howard, S., 'Dawdon in the "Third Period": The Dawdon dispute of 1929 and the Communist Party', *North East Labour History* 21, 1987, pp. 3–16
Hunt, B., *Northern Coalfields: Official Centenary History of the Northern League 1889–1989*. Skol Northern League Management Committee, 1989
Johnson, R.W. & Aughton, R., *The River Tyne, its Trade and Facilities*. Newcastle, 1930

Kelly & Co. Ltd., *Kelly's Directory of Durham*. 1894
Lapsley, G.T., 'Text of the Boldon Book', in Page, W. (ed.), 1905, pp. 327–42
Lawrence, A., 'Demonstration of rescue apparatus, Felling, August 31st. 1907', NEIMME, XXXV, 1907–8, pp. 210–30
Lawson, J., 'The influence of Peter Lee' in Bulmer, M., 1978, pp. 95–104
Lee, J., *Weardale Memories and Traditions*. Consett, 1950
Letch, H., *Birtley: Gleanings from the History of Birtley*. Newcastle, 1970
Lloyd, E., *History of the Crook and neighbourhood Co-operative Corn Mill, Flour and Provision Society Limited 1865–1915*. Pelaw, 1916
Ludlow, M. & Jones, L., *The Progress of the Working Classes 1832–67*. 1867
McGonigle, G.E.N. & Kirby, J., *Poverty and Public Health*. 1936
Meade, R., *The Coal and Iron Industries of the UK*. 1882
Milburn, G.E., 'The Census of worship of 1851', Durham Co. Local Hist. Soc. 17, 1974, pp. 3–20
Minchin, W.E., (ed.), *Industrial South Wales, 1750–1914*. 1969
Moran, L., *The History of Brandon Colliery 1856 to 1960*. Houghton-le-Spring, 1988
Moyes, W.A., *The Banner Book: a study of the banners of the Lodges of the Durham Miners Association*. Newcastle, 1974
NCB, *Report of the Committee on Roadway Conveyors*. 1955
——, *North East Coal Digest*. 1978–9
——, *North East Coal Digest*. 1980–1
——, *North East Coal Digest*. 1982–3
——, *North East Coal Digest*. 1986–7
——, *Drilling for Coal at Sea*.
——, *The Murton coking plant*.
——, *Durham Div. No 3 (SE Durham) Area, Horden Colliery*
Newsom, J., *Out of the Pit: A Challenge to the Comfortable*. Oxford, 1936
NHN, 'The Brancepeth Colliery Disaster', *Crook Wesleyan Methodist Magazine*, VII, 1896, No. 5
Norris, P., 'The Irish in Tow Law, Co. Durham, 1851 and 1871', Durham Co. Local History Soc. 33, 1984, pp. 41–70
Oxberry, J., *Gateshead District Aged Mine-workers' Homes. The Birth of the Movement. A Tribute to the Memory of Joseph Hopper*. Gateshead, 1924
Page, W., (ed.), *The Victoria County History of the County of Durham*. 1, 1905
Palmer, H., 'Notes on an electrical transmission plant at East Howle Colliery' TIME, III, 1891–2, pp. 271–7
Parkinson, G., *True Stories of Durham Pit Life*. 1912
Pattenden, D.W., 'The Origins of Seaham Harbour', The North East Industrial Archaeology Soc. 15, 1972, pp. 3–9
Peart, E., 'Bishop Auckland Co-operative Society' Durham Co. Local Hist. Soc., 13, 1970, pp. 8–21
Peel, R., *An Elementary Textbook on Coal Mining*. 1918
PEP, *(Political & Economic Planning) Industries Group 1936 Report on the British Coal Industry*.
Purdon, G.J., *Explosion at Easington! A Durham mine disaster remembered*. Beamish
——, *Twizell Pit Village*. Beamish
Raistrick, A., *Two Centuries of Industrial Welfare: The London (Quaker) Lead Company 1692–1905*. Buxton, 1977
Robson, D.A., (ed.), *The Geology of North East England*. Newcastle, 1980
Ross, T., *Jubilee History of the Felling Industrial Society Ltd. 1861 to 1911*. Pelaw, 1911
Sadler, S.A., 'Discussion' Darby, J.H., 1894–5, pp. 62–3
Seymour-Wood, E., 'The electrification of Murton Colliery, County Durham', TIME, XXXIX, 1910, pp. 226–43
Sharp, T., *Cathedral City: A Plan for Durham*. Durham, 1945

Sill, M., 'Deep coal mining in North East England in the 1980s', *Northern Economic Review*, 6, 1983, pp. 28–34
Smith, R., *Sea Coal for London. History of the Coal Factors in the London market*. 1961
Smith, W.V., 'The 1851 Census of Worship and the Irish immigration into County Durham', *Northern Catholic History*, 7, 1978, pp. 20–32
South Hetton Coal Co. Ltd, *South Hetton and Murton collieries*. Cheltenham, 1934
Spencer, J.R., *The Northern Pageant*. Newcastle, 1937
Steavenson, A.L., 'The Carboniferous limestone quarries of Weardale', TIME, XXII, 1901-2, pp. 115–23
——, 'On some experiments with the Lemielle ventilation at Page Bank Colliery', NEIMME, XVIII, 1868–9, pp. 63–9
Stobbs, A.W., *Memories of the LNER. South-west Durham*. Penrith, 1989
Sturgess, R.W., *Aristocrat in Business: The third Marquis of Londonderry as Coal Owner and Port Builder*. Durham Co. Local Hist. Soc., 1975
Surtees, H.C., *History of the parish and township of Evenwood and the parish of Eldon*. Mainsforth, 1923
Tantobie Co-operative Society, *A Short History of the Tantobie Co-operative Society Limited*. Pelaw, 1912
Tate, S., 'Winding, banking out and screening plant at East Hetton Colliery', TIME, I, 1889 , pp. 3–9
Taylor, W.N., 'Description of air-compressed machinery as applied to underground haulage etc. at Ryhope Colliery', NEIMME XXI, 1872, pp. 73–9
Teeside Chamber of Commerce *Souvenir of the Royal visit to Teeside*. Stockton,1930
The North East Housing Association Ltd, *25 Years of Housing 1935–1960*. Newcastle, 1960
Thornton, N.M., 'Endless-rope haulage at Pelton Colliery', TIME, XX, 1900–1, pp. 96–201
Townsend, P., Philimore, P. & Beattie, A., *Health and Deprivation: Inequality and the North*. 1988
Walker, G., 'George Harvey and Industrial Unionism', *North East Labour History* 17, 1983, pp. 21–4
Walton, J., *Calendar of the Greenwell Deeds*. Newcastle, 1927
Watkins, G., *The Steam Engine in Industry 2*. Ashbourne, 1979
Whellan, F., *History, Topography and Directory of the County Palatine of Durham*. 1894
Widdas, C.G., 'Westoe Colliery reconstruction', *Iron and Coal Trades Review*. Aug. 15, 1958, pp. 3–16
Williams, W.H., *Coal Combines in Durham*. Labour Research Dept., London, 1939
Wilson, A.S., 'The Origins of the Consett Iron Company, 1840–1864' *DUJ*, LXIV, 1972, pp. 90–102
Wolsingham Steel Co. Ltd., *The First Hundred Years*, Wolsingham, 1966
Wood, R., *West Hartlepool*. West Hartlepool, 1967
Wood, W.O., 1894–5 'The Murton coal washer', NEIMME, IX , pp. 42–6.
——, 'The Sussmann electric miners lamp', TIME, XXI, 1900–1, pp. 189–197
Woodcock, G., '"Radical Jack" John George Lambton, First Earl of Durham', *History Today*, IX, no. 1, 1959, pp. 3–12

7. Theses

Griffin, C.P., The Economic and Social Development of the Leicester and South Derbyshire Coalfield, Nottingham Univ. Ph D., 1969

Index

Page numbers in *italic* type refer to illustrations